Mediating with Picasso

**RELYING
ON YOUR
INHERENT CREATIVITY
WHEN YOU NEED IT
MOST**

Copyright © 2011 by Louise Neilson, MS.

All rights reserved.
Published in the United States by Brinkley Press

Grateful acknowledgment is made for permission to reprint The Creative Problem Solving: Thinking Skills Model from *Creative Leadership: Skills That Drive Change* by Gerard Puccio, Mary Murdock, and Marie Mance, © 2007 Sage Publications, Inc.

Library of Congress Cataloguing-in-Publication Data
Neilson, Louise

Mediating with Picasso: Relying on Your Inherent Creativity When You Need It Most / Louise Neilson

Includes bibliographical references and index.

ISBN 978-1-300-38635-3

Creativity. 2. Conflict management. 3. Mediation.
I. Neilson, Louise, 1944- II. Title.

Book design by Heidi Neilson.
All illustrations by Louise Neilson except where noted.
Back cover photograph by Alexander B. Craghead.

Mediating with Picasso

RELYING
ON YOUR
INHERENT CREATIVITY
WHEN YOU NEED IT
MOST

Conceived and Written by
Louise Neilson

Published by Brinkley Press, Damascus, OR
Printed by Lulu

Table of Contents

My Opening Statement 7

PART ONE—You as a Creative Person

    CHAPTER ONE: Background Information 13

    CHAPTER TWO: A Blinding Flash of the Obvious 31

    CHAPTER THREE: Barriers to Creative Thinking 59

    CHAPTER FOUR: Historical Attitudes Toward Creativity 87

PART TWO—You as a Creative Mediator

    CHAPTER FIVE: What's Your Style? 99

    CHAPTER SIX: What's Your Type? 111

    CHAPTER SEVEN: Values, Metaphors and Impartiality 133

PART THREE—Applications to Your Mediation Practice

    CHAPTER EIGHT: Picasso Meets the Red Queen 159

    CHAPTER NINE: Mediation as Improvisation 179

    CHAPTER TEN: In Defense of Creative Problem Solving 199

    CHAPTER ELEVEN: The Authors' Dialogue Creatively Continues 221

    CHAPTER TWELVE: Conclusion 237

Acknowledgements 243

Glossary 245

Chapter Notes 249

Bibliography 261

Index 271

About the Author 281

Most leaders don't work with oil paint, clay, or water colors. They create with the most complex medium of all—people.... Artists have it easy. Paint and clay don't go on strike ... don't stomp away in anger ... never need drug abuse counseling, or days off. People are so much more complicated than inanimate media. It takes tremendous effort and dedication to create with people—but the dividends can be phenomenal.

> Roger Firestien,
> *Leading on the Creative Edge*, p. 21.

My Opening Statement

You are a creative person and therefore a creative mediator! I say this as the only mediator in the country with a master's degree in creativity. Your inherent creativity is with you every time you take on the role of mediator to help others step out of their comfort zone and make unique mental connections to solve their problems. By being more aware of the extent of your own creativity, you can more consciously incorporate that innate ability as you mediate: more effectively "mediate with Picasso."

What does Picasso have to do with any of this? Young Pablo's talent was encouraged by his artist father, making Picasso one of very few creative children whose potential was not lost or buried as he grew up. When viewing Picasso's later expressionistic work, you might conclude that he was a scribbling painter who could not draw faces or the human form. But when you examine his early drawings you will see that Picasso knew what he was doing. As a young artist he diligently studied composition and could draw the human body with great accuracy. At an exhibition of children's work he attended when he was famous, Picasso quipped, "When I was their age I could draw like Raphael, but it has taken me a whole lifetime to learn to draw like them."[1]

The Picasso metaphor invokes the need to learn the mediation basics before trying risky strategies. Picasso's later work looked spontaneous and undisciplined precisely because he had mastered the necessary artistic skills before expanding the breadth of his artistic expression. Even then, Picasso filled entire notebooks with compositional studies for each of his major paintings. By the time he initiated his final product, he had rehearsed every paint stroke to the point that they appeared immediate and childlike.

The Picasso metaphor also evokes the innovative, genius

Below and above, outside and beyond the narrow walls with which violence wishes to enclose our human community, we must live with trust that creativity, divinely embedded in the human spirit, is always within reach. Like a seed in the ground, creative capacity lies dormant, filled with potential that can give rise to unexpected blossoms that create turning points and sustain constructive change.

> John Paul Lederach,
> *The Moral Imagination*, p. 173.

Picasso sitting next to you as your co-mediator; someone who opens up possibilities neither you nor the parties or clients ever even considered. The metaphor infers that after initial study and practice in the art of mediation, you more intuitively know what to say next, how to reframe issues, and how to guide the parties. With experience and new insights into your own inherent creativity, you gain the assurance to risk approaches you were never taught in Mediation 101, but intuitively know are the right things to do.

In one of my former lives I owned a ceramic tile business that produced handmade tiles for commercial and residential customers. Early on I was obsessed with making the perfect clay square. Eventually I learned that there was no such thing. Instead, each tile was practice for the next one. The same principle applies to mediation. There is no perfect mediation. Like Picasso's notebook of sketches, each mediation becomes practice for the next one. With each mediation, you practice being in the moment, maintaining a totally egoless focus on the parties. In doing so, you bring forth creative aspects of yourself appropriate to the situation.

Finally, *Mediating with Picasso* also works as a metaphor for dealing with the demanding and manipulative Picasso as one of the parties. By all accounts, in his personal life, Pablo was pretty much of a jerk. Those around him might have welcomed a safe place where they could have honestly expressed the negative affect he had on them. When you mediate with Picasso you bring forth those innate creative qualities in yourself appropriate for responding to equally difficult parties.

As Lederach so eloquently states, we must trust that creativity is always with us, that "embedded in our human spirits, always within reach ... creative capacity lies dormant, filled with potential that can give rise to unexpected blossoms that create turning points and sustain constructive change."[2] My purpose in writing *Picasso* is to convince you that your creativity *is* within you.

Some of you might be thinking, "I already trust in my inherent creativity." Good for you! However, I suspect that most of you are probably more tentative on the subject. Once you fully trust that your own dormant creativity is really there, you can validate its presence and potential within yourself. You will see it when you believe it.

> What is most intimate to us is most universal. The most personal struggles of an individual very likely mirror those of an entire group, indeed a whole culture ... There may well be significant aspects of an individuals' personal dilemmas which suggest directions for economic and social change in this country.
>
> Jane Driscoll,
> *Defense Workers Shift Gears*, p. 3.

Why is it important to mediate more creatively? It is important because whatever is most intimate is also most universal. Creativity is not only relevant but essential in conflict situations. Personal, societal, and cultural conflicts beg for more people of creativity, compassion, and self-awareness. Those who are able to bring peace into the lives of others as a way to bring about peace among nations.

In his famous 1945 quote, Einstein prophesied that "the unleashed power of the atom has changed everything save our modes of thinking, and thus we drift toward unparalleled catastrophes."[3] I think it is safe to say that since 1945 things have only gotten worse. The more you are able to put your inherent whole brain complex creative thinking to use the more you can initiate and sustain constructive change in your part of the world.

Einstein's new modes of thinking, aka creative thinking, have long been called for. Whatever is most intimate is indeed most universal. The world's dilemmas and increased rate of change make it essential, even critical, for people to learn new methods of solving problems.[4] As Bernard Mayer has stated in *Beyond Neutrality: Confronting the Crisis in Conflict Resolution*, the greatest challenge to the field of alternative dispute resolution and peacemaking is to find ways to reframe our vision; to think of ourselves and the work we do in a different way, to project our role more broadly and creatively.[5] To do that, we need to move beyond whatever assumptions, fears, and blocks hold us back.

This book is my contribution to the ongoing dialogue within the mediation community, which includes any of you who find yourself in the role of mediator. No matter how creative you currently think you are, my hope is that by the time you finish reading *Mediating with Picasso* you will be convinced you are more creative than you previously thought. My invitation is for you to learn more about yourself as a creative person and apply that understanding to the conflicts in your area of influence. Once you have a greater belief in your own creativity, you will respond more creatively to challenges facing the nation and the world, let alone the field of mediation.

I invite you to look beneath the surface of your own assumptions, to examine the limits you have accepted or created, to step outside your ideas about what you can and cannot do.

I invite you to mediate dangerously, to take the risk of exploring your own heart and spirit, and to test the limits of what is possible.

>Kenneth Cloke,
>*Mediating Dangerously: The Frontiers of Conflict Resolution*, pp. xiii-xiv.

CHAPTER ONE

Background Information

Creativity is an integral part of any mediation. Having received my mediation training before attending graduate school to study creativity, I was constantly aware of the commonalities between the two disciplines. I was especially startled by the similarities between the attributes of creative persons and those of people who self-select to become mediators. Way back then I thought to myself, "I should write a book about this."

Comments I made in grad school about these seemingly obvious connections were met with blank stares. The director of the program even asked, "Why are you interested in that law thing? There's no money in it." He could not fathom why I wanted to be involved in something as obscure as mediation when there was big money to be made in product innovation. Back in the late 1980s it was hard to describe what mediation was all about. "I know we don't get along, but why do you want us to meditate ... mitigate ... medicate?"

Nor could the director understand why I was interested in creativity as it applied to conflict resolution. Unfortunately, my idealistic response was, "I don't think the world needs yet another brand of soap." That was when I was sternly informed that Proctor and Gamble was one of the director's consulting clients.

Before graduate school I had been introduced to Creative Problem Solving (CPS) through a class at Portland State University. Armed with an old degree in elementary education, I began teaching drawing, pottery, and Creative Problem Solving to inner-city middle school Talented and Gifted (TAG) kids. About the same time, back then during the Cold War, I was involved with Educators for Social Responsibility where I was introduced to the concept of mediation. I immediately saw connections between the mediation process and Creative Problem Solving.

How the Brain Processes Information

Left Visual Field Right Visual Field

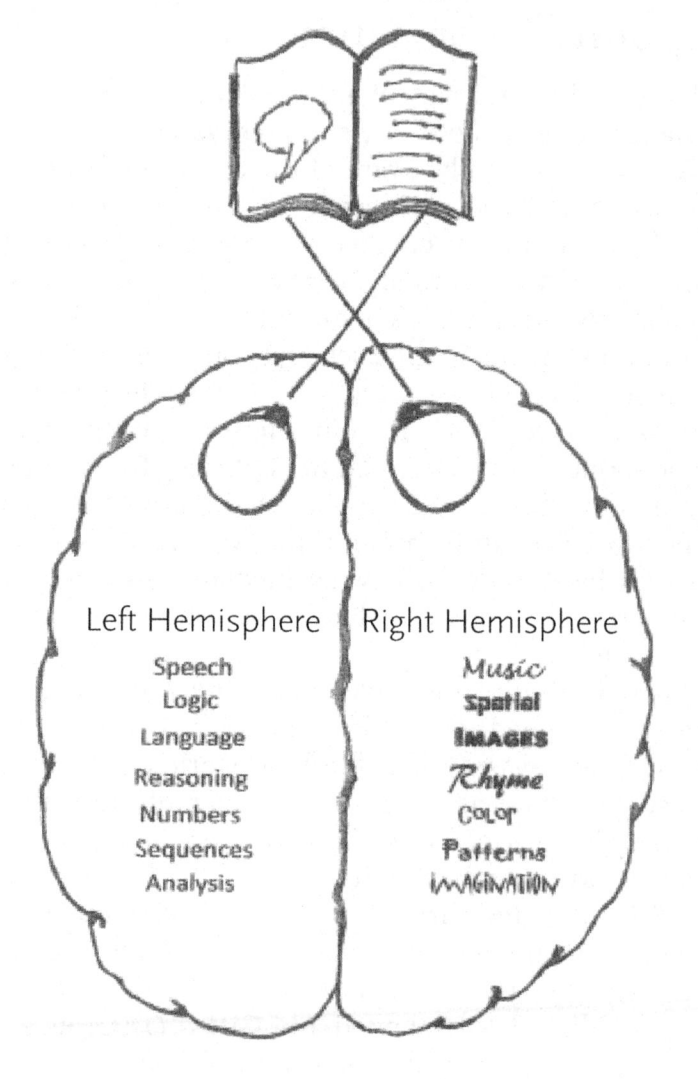

Left Hemisphere
Speech
Logic
Language
Reasoning
Numbers
Sequences
Analysis

Right Hemisphere
Music
Spatial
Images
Rhyme
Color
Patterns
Imagination

Gordon Dryden & Jeannette Vos,
The Learning Revolution, pp. 18-121.
Ned Herrmann, *The Creative Brain*, p. 14.

I was so intrigued by mediation's possibilities that I entered the certificate program in conflict resolution at Willamette University Law School's Center for Dispute Resolution in Salem, Oregon. Mornings found me working with very bright preteen TAG kids designing a one-size-fits-all wearable robot, or strategizing ways to have a no-risk food fight outside the principal's visual range. At noon I hopped in my car for my commute to the law school.

Because I was so enmeshed in actual creative problem solving, the *creative* process was front and center in my mind as I was introduced to *mediation* process. I was amazed by the glaringly apparent similarities between the two. Both processes were describing much the same thing, although using very different language.

Over the years I made several attempts to write a book connecting conflict and creativity, which always took the direction of being a *mediation* book about *creativity*. I found myself blocked by my own definition. I assumed my book had to look like every other conventional mediation book: linear, ponderous, and certainly without humor. There had to be a more creative way to present my observations and conclusions. Wait a minute! I could write a *creativity* book about *mediation!*

ABOUT THE BOOK ITSELF

As you have noticed by now, the text is on the right hand page. Quotes, graphs, drawings, and summaries of main concepts fill the left page. The inclusion of quotes from various creativity and mediation authors provides a way to include their views in the ongoing conversation. "Whole brain" learning research has found that by glancing over the left page as you read the right page text you engage your entire brain which helps you more efficiently store, recall, and later retrieve the information.

If it works for you, use the left page to pause and reflect on the perspectives presented. They also can be copied for use elsewhere. (Think refrigerator or bathroom mirror.) Routinely seeing them further encourages your subconscious learning.

Throughout *Picasso* you will be asked introspective open-ended questions. They are not rhetorical. They invite you into further thought and conversations on the various intersections of creativity and conflict resolution. Chapter Notes are found at the end rather than within the text, where they could be a distraction.

This is a creativity book for mediators, and for managers, teachers, counselors, and all others who are ...

- already self-acknowledged creative mediators.
- aspiring creative mediators.
- potentially creative mediators.

This book will ...

- increase your level of creativity.
- inform and foster awareness of your individual creative qualities.
- explore how your creative characteristics influence your mediation practice.
- offer creative methods and techniques to incorporate in mediation.

While readily available, they won't get in the way of your reading. There is also a glossary of some of the more obscure terms.

ABOUT THE *MEDIATING WITH PICASSO WORKBOOK*

The companion *Mediating with Picasso Workbook* is for those of you who are not yet convinced of your own creativity. In it are several exercises as well as thirteen creative self-assessment surveys that have been adapted or incorporated from a range of sources. Complete the assessments as you read *Picasso*. Then accumulate your results in the Creative Assessment Summary located in the *Workbook*. This Summary provides a mechanism for you to cumulatively validate, in your own experience, your new-found creativity. You will believe it when you see it!

A primary reason creativity is so hard to see is the belief that all creativity resides at the genius level of achievement. In *Picasso* I focus on the kind of everyday creativity you use when you manage a project, rearrange your furniture, plan your travel route, or mediate between people.

The various surveys allow and encourage you to become aware of your creative blocks and barriers. You can then more consciously and deliberately address those stubborn, self-imposed and self-defeating beliefs that you are not creative. The *Workbook* also provides space for you to respond to the introspective questions found in *Picasso*, and to review the concepts in *Picasso* you found most interesting, intriguing, and useful. As you do so, there is space for you to note these concept's applications in your own life.

What is really wonderful is that as you increase your *belief* in the reality of your own creativity, you concurrently increase your *level* of creativity. As you remove lingering barriers, you will be able to inform and support your growing awareness of your own creative attributes, style, and potential for creative leadership.

You *will* believe it when you see it!

NEW MEDIATORS

If you are a new mediator it is important that you stay within the lines of the essential mediation skills you initially learned. This includes maintaining your perceived neutrality, actively listening to the parties, validating appropriately, and separating the parties' issues from their interests. Like Picasso learning to draw, give

> The difference between a child's drawing and the childlike drawings of Picasso resides not only in Picasso's impeccable mastery of craft, but in the fact that Picasso had actually grown up, undergone hard experience, and transcended it.
>
> Stephen Nachmanovitch, *Free Play*, p. 125.

yourself time to internalize these basic skills. This will give you the experience necessary to mature into a competent and fully-functioning creative mediator.

When you observe or co-mediate with more experienced mediators, you might be surprised and actually critical of their behaviors. Unless they were trained by the same person or team as you were, they might proceed with the mediation in slightly different ways. Elements of their opening statement might sound unfamiliar. Their terminology might sound different, even wrong. But know that those Picasso-like creative behaviors are used only after those seasoned mediators became fully grounded in basic mediation concepts.

Finally, as a new mediator you naturally bring existing skills and abilities from other successful areas of your life. There is a tendency to want to superimpose them onto your mediation practice, blurring the lines between your established competencies and your emerging mediation skills. Mediators with a background in sales tend to sell. Teachers teach. Lawyers advise. Judges judge. I have a vivid memory of a newly retired judge, mediating his first volunteer case, pounding his fist on the table, repeatedly saying to the parties, "I strongly urge you ...!"

As a new practitioner, it is essential for you to set aside prior or potentially conflicting competencies for the sake of learning new ones in their "pure" form; like young Picasso learning to draw. Only after you have internalized a new repertoire of mediation tools, tactics and responses is it appropriate to re-integrate your previous competencies. This approach allows you to first develop your basic mediation skills before eventually beginning to mediate more creatively. Otherwise you will randomly and repeatedly cross the lines between competencies without even knowing where the lines are. As you gain experience you will be able to *choose* when and why to mediate with a Picasso mind.

Trust me, I'm the expert. I promise that after reading *Mediating with Picasso* and the companion *Workbook*, you will have expanded your realization of how creative you already are and increased the ways you can mediate—in a Picasso state of mind.

> To move our field forward, we have to give up or at least significantly modify some of the ways we have understood our work and approach to conflict.
>
> Bernard Mayer, *Beyond Neutrality*, p. 147.

MEDIATION AUTHORS ON CREATIVITY

Excellent mediation books are on the market to introduce the basic concepts necessary to help you develop technical skills. Some offer a range of conflict resolution theories. Mediation writers have long acknowledged the need for creativity in conflict resolution. Earlier writers have advocated broadening the creative roles mediators can play in conflict resolution processes,[1] even acknowledging that "... mediation also requires creativity."[2] In *Beyond Neutrality*, Bernard Mayer repeatedly mentions the need for creativity as he calls on mediators to adopt "a new way of thinking about your fundamental identity as a field and as practitioners within the field." Mayer further maintains "what disputants need from conflict resolvers is more than process: they need understanding, engagement, creativity, strength, wisdom, strategic thinking, confrontation, patience, encouragement, humor, courage ... qualities that are not only about process or substance."[3]

Authors of mediation essays and books describe a variety of attributes needed to be considered a competent mediator. These qualities include tolerance for ambiguity, and whole brained and lateral thinking, the same attributes found in people that the experts designate as "creative." Lang and Taylor express the need for mediators to think strategically while being fully present in the moment, and "to influence the future while simultaneously ignoring it."[4] The creativity literature refers to this whole brained thinking as being in "flow"[5] and "bisociative thinking."[6] Another writer[7] emphasizes the importance of a mediator using "lateral thinking," a term first coined by creativity expert Edward de Bono.[8] Among the most eloquent conclusions is that although "preparation is required to exercise ingenuity and judgment ... imagination is the connective tissue."[9]

Mediators have been described as stage managers, directors, court jesters, and from the Native American tradition, Coyote or trickster.[10] Mediators *are* benevolent tricksters, shape shifters using their creativity to see the parties' issues in a new light and deliver them in a favorable package to the other party, using their inherent talent as a trickster, along with creativity and intuitive understanding, to bring peace into the lives of others.[11] Both creativity and imagination "... embrace the possibility that there exist untold possibilities capable at any moment to move beyond the narrow parameters of what is commonly accepted and perceived

Mental Snow Globe

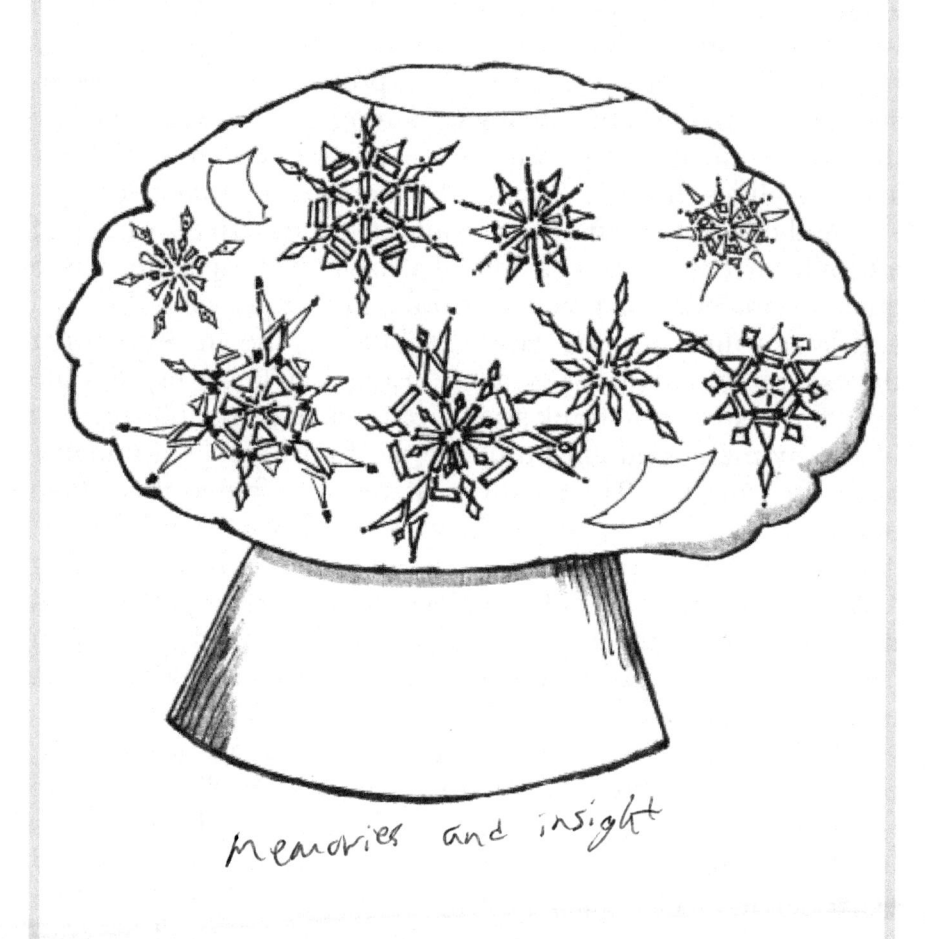

memories and insight

22 | MEDIATING WITH PICASSO

as the narrow and rigidly defined range of choices."[12]

Finally, Lang and Taylor express their hope that the field of mediation can creatively respond to the concepts and methods they developed and described in their book, *The Making of a Mediator*. They invited further professional dialogue about these and other ideas that may occur to their readers.[13] They often end with recommendations for changes in the field. *Picasso* begins where these books leave off. My unique background in the seemingly separate field of creativity brings new insights into the discussion from a wide range of authors and disciplines. *Picasso* synthesizes knowledge, models, and tools from cognitive and positive psychology, whole brain research, metaphors, and education as well as creativity research. It then applies them to the field of mediation.

Mediating with Picasso is my response to that call for further professional dialogue about mediation theories and approaches, as well as the future of conflict engagement and mediation. This creativity book about mediation is not only for those of you not yet convinced of your inherent creativity. It is also for those of you who entertain the notion that you *are* a creative person and who are willing to give yourself permission to become even *more* creative in your mediation practice. It is my contribution to the call for the development of higher levels of self-reflection, self-awareness, and authenticity in the art of mediation: higher levels of creativity.

SNOWFLAKES AND BLIND SPOTS

Throughout *Picasso* you will read about physiological, neurological, and cognitive theoretical aspects of creative thinking. Some will seem more attractive than others. My intention is to provide a kaleidoscope of the different facets of creativity for you to layer over your own current knowledge and beliefs—some of which may need to be undone.

As you read *Picasso*, pay close attention to random thoughts that surface, forgotten incidents, or things you read or heard long ago. My Snow Globe Theory addresses these kinds of memories. As you suddenly remember something, you are turning your mental snow globe upside down and shaking it, causing that memory to fall, often accompanied by other loosely associated memories. In these moments, your intuition is providing you

Fourth Grade Memories

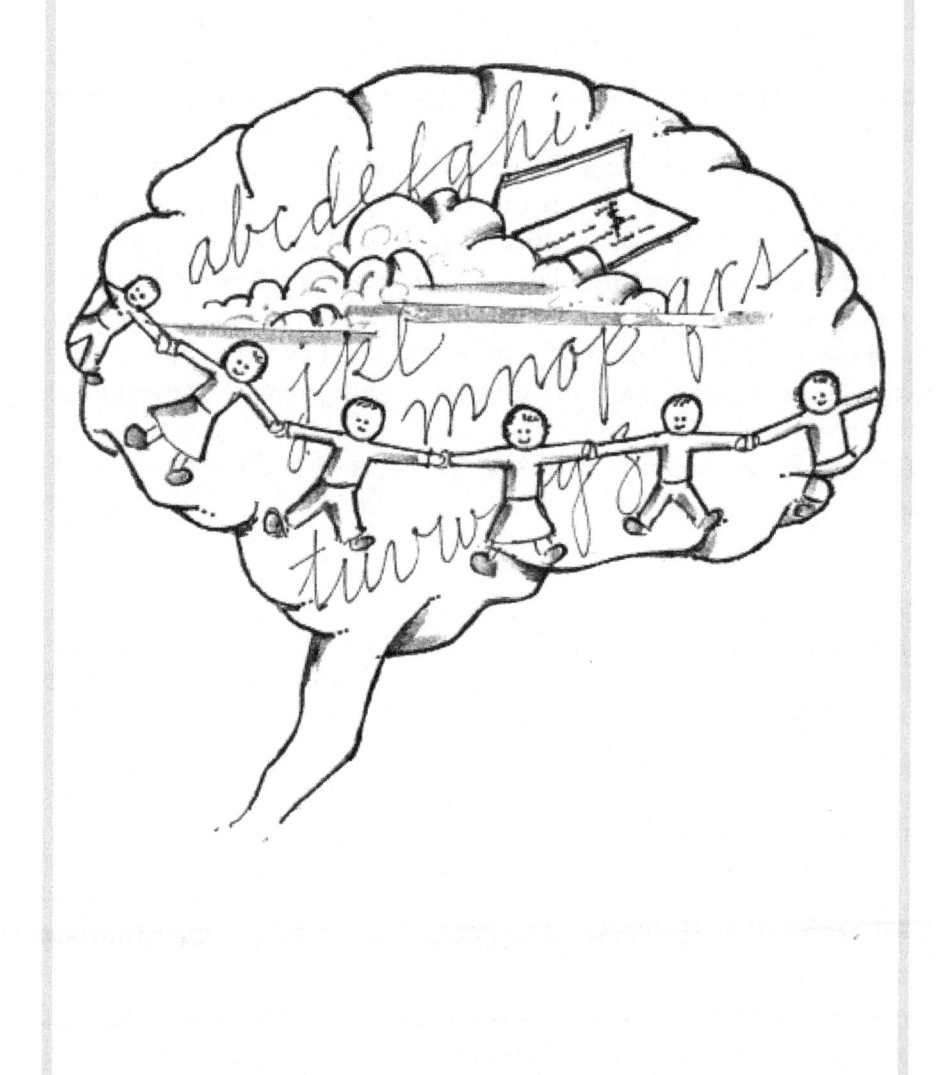

with both memory and insight.

For example, when I am randomly reminded of something, I have learned to not just dismiss the memory, but instead to rummage around the snowflakes to find the exact mental connection being presenting to me. All this, however, takes place in an instant. Sometimes snowflakes of memory have to settle for a second or two before I can determine their exact relevance. For example, when I suddenly remember my fourth grade teacher, Mr. Yoswick, I think, "Cloud formations? No.... How to write checks? No.... Ah, he taught us to honor the cultural differences among students in our class." Bingo!

When this happens to you as you read *Picasso*, pause and ask yourself, "Why did I remember that particular thing? What is its connection to what I'm reading right now?" Then write down your responses alongside your recorded memories.

My Snow Globe Theory is a metaphor for insight and intuition, scientifically explained through neuroscience's discovery of the part of your brain called the reticular formation. This tangle of tiny neurons extends from the top of the spinal cord through the brainstem to deep within the cerebrum, your brain's center for cognition and the area dedicated to high level thought like rational decision making.[14]

But that's not all. Although your brain's various systems are triggered by emotions, all incoming information must first get through your reticular formation's activating system before it is forwarded to the cerebrum. Your Reticular Activating System (RAS) pays attention to some things while ignoring others. Your attention involves a number of distinct processes, from filtering out perceptions to balancing multiple perceptions to attaching emotional significance to them.[15]

Your Reticular Activating System also has direct lines of command to major areas of your cortex and the brainstem, as well as down the spinal cord where it influences sensory and motor systems throughout your body. It awakens selected nervous circuits and desensitizes others.[16] Only then does your brain "turn on" thoughts, emotions or both. The cerebrum is unresponsive unless the RAS sends the signal to begin the data processing.[17] That's where "Ahas!" originate. They're snowflakes!

So pay attention to those obscure mental connections as they occur. Your intuition is connecting a past experience to some-

> Your creative potential will be enhanced through your awareness of the principles that inform your practice, together with an open receptive beginner's mind.
>
> Michael D. Lang & Alison Taylor,
> *The Making of a Mediator*, p. xiv.

thing relevant in the moment. Note your associations *as* you become aware of them, even during mediations. Too many valuable creative ideas are lost because they were not written down for future reference. Note your "Ahas!" as you come across them in your reading here. Don't wait. *Picasso* is meant to be used, not just read.

Time for a simple creative exercise. Clasp your hands together. Which thumb is on top? (My right thumb is always on top, so that *must* be the correct answer.) Now unclasp your fingers, rotate your palms slightly, re-clasping your hands so the opposite thumb is on top. How does that feel? Could you readily make the switch, or did you resist? What intuitive message did you receive from the experience? Workshop participants often report that their new hand position is awkward. Like a new idea, it is uncomfortable. It challenges conventional thinking, and in fact, is "downright stupid!"

Here is what's happening. Your brain's off switch causes mental blind spots, called "scotomas." These blind spots filter out or completely reject information that doesn't fit; information incongruent or contrary to what you already "know," including clasping your hands in the "wrong" way.

I once owned a car with the ignition switch next to the gear shift knob rather than on the steering column. To pull the key out of the ignition I had to put the car in reverse. To put the car in reverse I had to put my thumb on the top of the knob while my first and second fingers wrapped around each side of the knob from below. Then I had to simultaneously push *down* on the gear knob with my right thumb while pulling *up* on a ring below the knob with my fingers. Try it. It is a very awkward, claw-like position. It took months for this gesture to become routine, during which time, my *car* was stupid! Of course, after it became routine, I would get into a *normal* car and not be able to *find* the ignition. It was in the *wrong* place.

That is how it might feel to read some of the ideas presented in *Picasso*. A concept does not fit, it is uncomfortable, it challenges conventional thinking, and in fact, it's downright stupid! When you find yourself resistant to new ideas presented here, un-clasp your mind, regain your curiosity as well as your impartiality, and at least *consider* that there might be some validity to the concept. Challenge your entrenched belief systems as they reveal them-

The Nine Dot Puzzle

• • •

• • •

• • •

Directions:
Without lifting your pencil, draw four straight lines that cross all nine dots.

James Adams,
Conceptual Blockbusting, pp. 29-31.

selves. Otherwise they remain cognitive blind spots that prevent you from thinking "outside the box," other than what might just turn out to be valuable information.

THINKING OUTSIDE THE BOX

The term "outside the box" has become shorthand for creative thinking. It was originally coined as the answer to the Nine Dot Puzzle, shown on the left.[18] The challenge presented in the puzzle is to draw, without lifting your pencil, four straight lines that cross all nine dots. Try it before looking on page 7 of the *Workbook* to see the solution. It is harder than you think.

Here is what is happening. As you attempt to solve the puzzle, your brain's scotomas make it difficult to see beyond the "box" the imaginary boundary the dots represent. To solve the Nine Dot Puzzle you need to literally think outside the box the nine dots creates. Try it again here or in the *Workbook*. Solving the puzzle takes deliberate and continued practice. Does your brain have a difficult time overcoming this unconscious boundary constraint, even though it is not presented as part of the challenge? Even knowing the solution, does your scotoma still want to kick in?

Sometimes it is appropriate, and even necessary, to mediate outside the box. Experienced mediators will tell you privately about behaviors, responses, methods, and techniques they incorporated into their mediations that they certainly did not learn in basic training. There are those who tell stories, bring food to the mediation, doodle, remain silent throughout, or use any number of other unorthodox outside the box strategies. (I admit to having done all of these.)

Case in point: as the four male thirty-something housemates began a discussion of their landlord/tenant dispute, they kept pausing and glancing in my direction. After a quick Snow Globe search of possible reasons, I reflected my observation back to them. Then I innocently asked if I needed to be the first person in the room to say "fuck." They looked at each other, sheepishly agreed, and then continued with their discussion, no longer self-conscious that the prim-looking middle-aged female sitting with them might be offended by their language.

That's mediating with Picasso.

Traits that reveal that which is most characteristic of the creative person:

- They are actualizing their creative potentialities.
- They have become the persons they were capable of becoming.
- They are not preoccupied with impressions they make on others or demands that others make on them.
- They are freer to set their own standards and to achieve them in their own fashion.
- They are perhaps the prototype of the person of strong ego, the person of will and deed.
- They are confident of themselves and basically self-accepting.
- To an unusual degree they are able to recognize and give expression to most aspects of inner experience and character.
- They are able to be more fully themselves and realize their own ideals.

Donald MacKinnon,
Architects, Personality Types, and Creativity,
pp. 175-289.

CHAPTER TWO

A Blinding Flash of the Obvious

"Mediators should be considered a distinct group of creative people!"

That was my Blinding Flash of the Obvious as a mediator studying creativity. This BFO occurred as I read about a study done in the early 1960s on creativity in architects. Researcher Donald MacKinnon[1] theorized that architects were a special group of creative individuals; those who he predicted "revealed that which is most characteristic of a creative person." MacKinnon concluded that architects must be artists (right brained) if their designs "are to give delight." On the other hand, architects must also be engineers (left brained) if their designs are to be technologically sound and efficiently planned. With that in mind, MacKinnon began a study to measure the differences in the degree to which architects had maximized and realized their creative potential. (Notice MacKinnon was not measuring their artistic or spatial abilities.) He conducted a battery of tests, surveys, and inventories to measure the following:

- The nature of the individual's socialization and his interpersonal behavior.
- The level of richness or complexity of his psychological development.
- The degree of personal soundness or psychological health he manifested.

Here is what MacKinnon[2] wrote in the early sixties when most architects were men, so there is room to forgive him for his non-inclusive language. Of the most creative architects, he concluded:

> What is most impressive ... is the degree to which they have actualized their creative potentialities. They have

Two Kinds of Creativity

BIG

C

Special Talent Creativity

Associated with great tangible achievements.

The type we **generally** associate with genius or higher level creativity.

little

c

Self-Actualizing Creativity

Acknowledges the potential for creativity and self-actualization in *everyone*.

Adapted from Abraham Maslow,
Toward a Psychology of Being, pp. 153-160.

become in large measure the persons they were capable of becoming. Since they are not preoccupied with the impression they make on others or the demands that others make on them, they are freer ... to set their own standards and to achieve them in their own fashion.... Their behavior is guided by aesthetic values and standards which they have set for themselves and of their ideals. They are perhaps the prototype of the person of strong ego, the man of will and deed. Confident of themselves and basically self-accepting, they are to an unusual degree able to recognize and give expression to most aspects of inner experience and character and thus are able to more fully be themselves and to realize their own ideals.

It was while reading the results of MacKinnon's research that I had my BFO: that experienced dedicated mediators, as a group, exhibit these same traits in their socialization and interpersonal behavior, in the richness and complexity of their psychological development, and their degree of mental health. I maintain that without these traits they could not be effective mediators.

Concurrent with MacKinnon's 1960's study on creativity in architects, the field of creativity was beginning to come into its own. Abraham Maslow[3] was developing his now famous concept of the hierarchy of needs, with self-actualization at the top. Maslow concluded that creativity was _synonymous_ with self-actualization and positive mental health! With Maslow, creativity began to lose its centuries-old association with mental illness and/or mental defect. (More on this later in Chapter Four.)

Maslow also distinguished between two different kinds of creativity. He called the first kind special talent creativeness, and associated it with great tangible achievements, the type we generally associate with genius or higher level creativity. I think of this as "Big C" creativity. The second kind, which I think of as "little c," and which Maslow named self-actualizing creativity, acknowledges the potential for creativity and self-actualization in everyone. Self-actualizing creativity stresses the person, not only their achievements. Maslow maintained that this second kind of creativity is an ever-increasing move toward unity and integration, a synergy within a person. He described self-actualizing creativity as an inherent, fundamental human characteristic synonymous with mental health; "a potentiality given to all or most human beings at birth, which most often is lost or buried or inhibited as

Maslow's general assessment of more creative, self-actualized people:

- Accepting of themselves, others, and human nature
- Having a deep connection with all humankind
- Capable of detachment from their own culture, and objectively compare cultures
- Tolerant of and even liking ambiguity
- Appreciating humor but having a more thoughtful, philosophical sense of humor, constructive rather than destructive
- Being problem-centered (not self-centered)
- Having less need for praise or popularity
- Having a philosophy, a mission in life
- Enjoy work toward achieving a goal as much as the goal itself
- Patient with others, for the most part
- Strongly ethical and moral in individual ways, but not necessarily in conventional ways
- Able to handle stress
- Tending to do most things creatively, without necessarily possessing great talent

Abraham Maslow,
The Farther Reaches of Human Nature,
pp. 308-309.

the person gets acculturated."⁴

Maslow acknowledged the potential for creativity and self-actualization in everyone. He did not mean people ascended his self-actualization ladder from the struggle for survival to a utopian place and then stayed there. Even self-actualizing people eventually get hungry.

According to Maslow, self-actualizing people are mentally healthy individuals who live fully productive lives, and who tend to approach all aspects of their lives in a flexible, creative fashion. These individuals may or may not be brilliantly creative in a specialized area; they do not need to be.

Maslow⁵ wrote that his research subjects:

> ... had put opposites together in such a way as to make me realize that regarding (them) as contradictory and mutually exclusive is itself characteristic of a lower level of personality development. They are all integrators, able to bring separates and even opposites together into unity. Such people can see the fresh, the raw, the concrete, the ideographic, as well as the generic, the abstract ... the categorized and the classified.

Like MacKinnon's conclusions about creative architects, Maslow concluded that creative people "were more 'natural' and less controlled and inhibited in their behavior, which seemed to flow out more easily and freely and with less blocking and self-criticism."⁶ Maslow compiled quite a number of specific self-actualizing creative traits. Some are listed below. As you read through the descriptions consider how many times you think to yourself, "So do I!" I contend that they are also qualities found in creative mediators.

Years ago I faced the crowded hall at my first mediation conference with my usual apprehension. As a short person I dreaded having to get myself, my conference materials, and my cup of coffee past the gauntlet of waiting elbows and backpacks. But this time it was different. Instead of being poked in the shoulders and the back of my head, individual mediators parted slightly allowing me to pass unjostled. I was so amazed that I made two more trips through the crowd to wallow in this new experience! Even as they were absorbed in their own conversations and distractions, they remained responsive to the needs of those around them. That experience always comes to my mind as a tangible example

> One practical consequence of positivity's mind-broadening powers is enhanced creativity. A broad mind changes the way you think and act in a wide range of circumstances. When you see more, more ideas come to mind, more actions become possible.
>
> Barbara Fredrickson, *Positivity*, p. 59.

of the subtle impact a group of self-actualizing people can have on the lives of others.

Maslow found that self-actualizing people tend not to need, seek, or even enjoy publicity, fame, honors, popularity, applause, status, prestige, or even wealth. They do not need to be loved by everyone. They get great pleasure from knowing courageous, honest, and effective people. They generally pick out their own small number of causes, rather than responding to advertising or other people's expectations. Their fighting is problem-centered, for the sake of setting things right, not as an excuse for hostility, paranoia, grandiosity, authority, or rebellion. They manage to somehow simultaneously love the world as it is while striving to improve it.

Maslow observed that self-actualizing persons tend to be unafraid of, and even attracted by the unknown, mystery, and unsolved problems. They enjoy bringing about law and order in chaotic, messy or confused situations. They try to free themselves from illusions; to courageously look at the facts. Self-actualizing people tend to feel that every person should have an opportunity to develop to their highest potential, to have a fair chance, to have equal opportunity. They enjoy taking on responsibilities, which they handle very well. They uniformly consider their work to be worthwhile, important, and even essential. As you read though these, ask yourself how many of these self-actualizing traits did you see in yourself? These attributes are listed in the *Workbook* in survey form to allow you to do a more thorough self-assessment.

POSITIVITY

Maslow's theories have found research-based empirical support from a recent branch of psychology, logically called 'positive psychology.' This branch seeks to find and nurture genius and talent, and to make normal life more fulfilling. Martin Seligman, considered the father of positive psychology, asserted that psychology had over time unwittingly adopted a disease model, concerning itself primarily with alleviating human suffering. He maintained that psychology's intense focus on reducing negativity and its attendant damage eclipsed virtually everything else. Martin Seligman pointed out that little scientific research was devoted to discovering how to call forth what makes life worth living.[7]

Words That Reflect Positivity

alert	amazed	amused
appreciative	awe	closeness
confident	content	curious
elevated	encouraged	fun-loving
glad	grateful	happy
hopeful	inspired	interested
joyful	love	optimistic
peaceful	proud	self-assured
serene	silly	thankful
trust	uplifted	wonder

Barbara Fredrickson, *Positivity*, pp. 142-143.

The term 'positivity' is deliberately broad. As described in the book, *Positivity*,[8] it includes positive meanings and attitudes that trigger positive emotions, heart rhythms and body chemistry, muscle tension and facial expressions, your resources and relationships. The ten most commonly reported forms of positivity are: joy, gratitude, serenity, interest, hope, pride, amusement, inspiration, awe, and love.

In controlled experiments positivity has been assessed by tracking the electrical signals within certain facial muscles. Precisely placed sensors measure the tiny electrical signals in the muscles that pull your lip corners up and the muscle that wrinkles the skin around your eyes. These signals are measured long before they are strong enough to create any recognizable facial expression. When "both sets of muscles are firing in tandem these two facial muscles forecast flexible and broadened attention captured by computerized tests that measure people's responses in milliseconds. Your smile, then, quite literally opens you. In the moments you are smiling, you are more receptive, more able to see the big picture."[9]

A positive and open mindset draws you (and your parties) out to explore and interact with the world in more unexpected ways. Each time you do, you learn new things. Positivity creates new connections in your brain, expanding your Reticular Activating System so you have the new information available to you later. There are vast implications of increased positivity to mediation. Indeed, it may be why mediation works at all.

An amazing example of the shift in thinking was once provided to me by a non-profit board furious with their executive director for taking another job. They initially expressed a range of negative emotions over her departure: anger, contempt, disgust, fear and stress. Basically, they wanted her to stay and felt betrayed by her departure. She had done so much for the organization that they didn't know how they were going to replace her. I asked for examples of her contributions. As they reminisced about her wonderful accomplishments they began expressing more positive feelings, including gratitude for her hard work and pride in the results. The board members' attitudes changed so completely that by the end of the meeting they voted to send her a bouquet of flowers to wish her well and thank her for her work on behalf of the organization! The situation was the same, only their attitude

> The brain stores information by making great use of associations. Every person's brain has an association cortex. It can link up like with like, from different memory banks. Learning to store information in patterns and with strong association is probably the first step toward developing your brain's untapped ability.
>
> Gordon Dryden & Jeannette Vos,
> *The Learning Revolution*, pp. 127-129.

had changed.

Positivity researcher Barbara Fredrickson,[10] sounding a lot like Maslow, maintains that ...

> ... among our birthrights as humans is the experience of the subtle and fleeting pleasant feelings of positivity. It comes in many forms and flavors. Think of the times you feel connected to others and loved; when you feel playful, creative, or silly; when you feel blessed and at one with your surroundings; when your soul is stirred by the sheer beauty of existence; or when you feel energized and excited by a new idea or hobby. Positivity reigns whenever positive emotions—like love, joy, gratitude, serenity, interest, and inspiration—touch and open your heart.

Are creative mediators successful because they are more positive in their outlooks? Or are they successful because they bring more positivity into the lives of the parties? Is positivity a means toward self-actualization? Or is positivity what self-actualization looks like?

The research on positivity has found that positivity actually "changes how your mind works. Positivity doesn't just change the contents of your mind, trading bad thought for good ones; it also changes the scope or boundaries of your mind. It widens the span of possibilities that you see ... you benefit from positivity's broader mindscape several ways."[11] One of the ways you might benefit from the broader mindscape is to expand your view of yourself as a creative mediator.

BRAIN RESEARCH

Breakthroughs in neurophysiology provide valuable new insights into how your brain processes information. Both sides of your brain are linked by an electronic and chemical relay system that allows it to work in an integrated way.[12] Your brain's switching system constantly balances incoming messages, linking together the concrete, logical messages with abstract pictures. When you think of someone you know, for example, the right brain pictures their face while the left brain remembers their name.

Based on the latest research scientists now conclude that the hemispheres of the brain work together for all cognitive tasks, even if there are functional asymmetries. As a highly integrated system, it is rare that one part of the brain works individually.

Luigi's Notes on Creativity

Creativity is a multi-faceted phenomenon.
Everyone is creative.
Creativity is relevant.
Creativity can cause conflict.
Creativity can resolve conflict.

Aspects of Creativity
Person
Process
Product
Press / Environment

There are some tasks—such as recognizing the faces and producing speech—that are dominated by a given hemisphere, but most require that the two hemispheres work at the same time.[13]

Both creative thinking and mediation involve that same complex thinking. When you mediate, you simultaneously function from both sides of your brain. As you listen to the parties, you impartially take in information while simultaneously assessing, weighing, discerning the intent of what you are hearing. Even assuming that somehow both parties can be right is very creative thinking. This is the same type of creative thinking that you share with architects, considered to be among the most creative people.

BASIC CONCEPTS ABOUT CREATIVITY

"Father Guido Sarducci" appeared some years ago on Saturday Night Live as a professor at what he called the Five Minute University. As he explained to the audience, he only taught those things the students would remember five years later anyway. For example, in economics the only thing he taught was "supply and demand." In his Spanish class he only taught "Como esta usted?"

From Guido's concept of the Five Minute University I have developed my own Luigi Chat. These are the basic concepts about creativity that everyone should know, and the only ones you will need to remember anyway. Creativity is a multi-faceted phenomenon. Everyone is creative. Creativity is relevant. Creativity can cause conflict. Creativity can resolve conflict.

Here is a brief overview of the classic creativity theories and perspectives. Creativity researcher E. P. Torrance[14] concluded that your creativity involves three elements: your inherent abilities, the extent to which you develop your creative skills, and your motivation to continue to improve them. Creativity occurs where your abilities, skills, and motivations come together. For example, where your inherent ability to mediate meets your skills and motivation to improve that ability. Note that your intrinsic aptitude has to be there. As much as I might be motivated to improve my singing skills, my basic ability to hear pitch just isn't there.

Yet another area of creativity research includes the creative person, creative process, creative product and creative "press" or environment. Dimensions of the creative person include person-

Attributes of a Creative Person

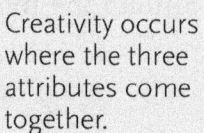

Creativity occurs where the three attributes come together.

Skill: Can be increased by learning.

Motivation: Can be increased by changing habits and attitudes, and overcoming blocks to your own creativity.

Ability: Needs to be recognized in yourself and others, honored and used.

Adapted from E. Paul Torrance,
The Search for Satori and Creativity, p. 12.

ality, intellect, traits, attitudes, values and behavior.[15] This whole chapter focuses on you as a creative person. The creative process includes the divergent (idea generation) and convergent (decision making) stages of creative thinking that anyone engages in when overcoming obstacles or achieving a goal. By definition, mediation is a creative process. (Chapter Ten delves into creative processes.) Creative products include the characteristics and outcomes of new thoughts, inventions, designs, or systems. Your mediated agreements are examples of creative products. The creative "press" is the relationship between people, environment, situation, and its effect on creativity. As mediator, you provide a creative environment by fostering positivity, safety and hope during your opening statement, especially by co-establishing with the parties the guidelines to be followed during the mediation session.

Still another facet of the multi-faceted phenomenon called creativity involves these four attributes: fluency, flexibility, originality, and elaboration. These become apparent when you are generating ideas. Imagine yourself for a moment among a group of people asked to generate ideas about "how to get from here to there." If you are among those who are strong in *fluency* you might come up with a large number of ways, such as walking, running, skipping, jumping, jogging, wandering, meandering, strolling and crawling.

If you are strong in *flexibility* you may not have as *many* ideas for how to get from here to there, but your ideas would cover a wider range of categories of possibilities, like swim, sky dive, ride a dolphin, drive a car/truck, row a boat, or take a plane/train/bus/ship.

If you are among those who score high on *originality* you tend to come up with ideas the others have not thought of, including dream, dogsled, beam yourself aboard, time travel, or add a "t" to "here."

Lastly, if you are among those in the brainstorming group who are strong in *elaboration* you might have still fewer ideas, but the ones you have are rich in detail: ride on the back of a giant turtle wearing scuba gear, hitchhike with a truck-load of cows, or ride in a hot air balloon taking lots of pictures that get published, and made into a bestselling coffee table book.

Approaches to Creativity

- Fluency—having lots of ideas
- Flexibility—involving different categories of ideas
- Originality—having unusual ideas, the statistical infrequency of someone else coming up with the same idea
- Elaboration—describing the intricacies of the idea in detail

J.P. Guilford, *Way Beyond the I.Q.*, pp. 33-65.

AMBIGUITY

Ambiguity involves the ability to understand inexplicable, obscure or indistinct things in two or more possible ways. Both creative thinking and mediation, especially cross-cultural mediations, involve complex thinking and a tolerance for ambiguity. This kind of thinking is the result of associating two incompatible frames of reference, resulting in a clash between two mutually incompatible contexts. The classic one-liners on the subject include "jumbo shrimp" and "military intelligence."

Arthur Koestler coined the term "bisociation" to distinguish this creative thinking from routine, non-ambiguous thinking. Bisociation describes what happens during those moments when two opposing thoughts are simultaneously held in the brain.[16] For example, when a reporter asked Gandhi what he thought of Western civilization he replied, "I think it would be a good idea." Bisociation describes the collision of those two contexts—the reporter's and Gandhi's—as something both unexpected and totally logical, but with a logic not usually applied to the reporter's type of question.

Koestler's bisociation can be explained by neuroscience. When your left brain is engaged, it functions at the awake "beta" wave length, actively transmitting and receiving at the rapid rate of 13-25 cycles per second. Concurrently the right side is functioning in the slower "alpha" wave or relaxed alertness state, at a steady 8-12 cycles a second. The methodical alpha brain waves bring a feeling of relaxation and well-being, as well as concentrated alertness. Inspiration, creativity, heightened memory, increased concentration, and the ability to quickly assimilate facts are all derived from alpha wave activity.[17] When you mediate, both alpha and beta waves are simultaneously engaged. This might be when you are bisociating; concurrently holding two opposing thoughts in your mind, "working with objective and subjective information simultaneously."[18]

OPPOSING CREATIVE TRAITS

Finally, here is a look at your creativity from yet another perspective. Based on interviews with complex creative thinkers, creativity researcher Csikszentmihalyi[19] expanded Maslow's assertion that self-actualizing creative persons lose "their separateness and oppositeness."[20] Again, it correlates to positivity, when you are

> For self-actualizing people,... the ordinary or conventional dichotomy between work and play is transcended totally. That is, there is certainly no distinction between work and play.
>
> Abraham Maslow,
> *The Farther Reaches of Human Nature*,
> p. 304.

more able to broaden your view of yourself. The boundaries that separate "me" from "you" begin to fade from view. As they do, new possibilities for connection emerge.[21]

Csikszentmihalyi concluded there are ten pairs of integrated yet apparently opposing traits present in creative individuals. While not all of these conflicting traits are necessarily found in the same person or mediator, these traits may be the most telling descriptors of creative people. Further, those who can operate from both ends of most of these polarities also fit the idea of a "little c" creative person.

1. Energy and Rest

Csikszentmihalyi found that creative individuals have a great deal of physical energy, but they also can be quietly at rest. They can work long hours, with great concentration, while projecting a sense of freshness and enthusiasm. Their energy is internally generated, under their own control, rather than controlled by calendars, clocks, or external schedules. When necessary, their energy can be laser focused and they can lose all track of time. It might be why you might start a mediation with low energy yet you can come away more energized than when you began.

2. Wise and Childlike

These opposing traits bring to mind Picasso's expert ability to draw like a child. "Wise" here is not equated with being "smart," but more with Maslow's "highest maturity that includes a child-like quality … their innocence of perception and expression was combined with a sophisticated mind."[22] Creative individuals tend to be at once sophisticated and naïve. Their wisdom is balanced with a childlike perspective. This does not mean you must be a genius. The IQ range of most creative people is around 120-130. The window of creativity closes if the IQ is much higher or lower.[23]

3. Playful and Disciplined

Csikszentmihalyi's third paradoxical trait refers to the related combination of responsibility and irresponsibility. Distinct from being childlike, a playfully light attitude is typical of creative individuals. But this playfulness does not go very far without its antithesis, a quality of doggedness, endurance, and perseverance.

Having a complex personality means being able to express the full range of traits that are potentially present in the human repertoire but usually atrophy because we think that one or the other pole is "good," whereas the other extreme is "bad."

> Mihaly Csikszentmihalyi,
> *Creativity: Flow and the Psychology of Discovery and Invention*, p. 57.

Here again the left and right brains are operating in tandem. Although I know that they are on duty and all business during a mediation session, I dread those times I am called on to facilitate a meeting of off-duty mediators who would rather horse around. Are you in this group?

4. Fantasy and Reality

Creative people favor reality-based fantasy; they are original without necessarily being bizarre. They alternate between imagination and fantasy on one hand, and a down-to-earth sense of reality on the other. Again, this implies the use of both brain hemispheres. When you mediate you are accessing both sides of your brain by: 1) assisting the parties in becoming more imaginative within the confines of their conflict while 2) helping them stretch their mental boundaries regarding possible solutions.

5. Extraversion and Introversion

This trait refers to the ability to exhibit opposite tendencies on the continuum between extraversion and introversion, allowing simultaneous expression of both traits. (Personality types are examined further in Chapter Six.) Even if you are an extraverted mediator, are you still comfortable with silence if that is what the parties need? If you are an introverted mediator, do you still find that you are comfortable sustaining prolonged conversations with the parties?

6. Humble and Proud

As a creative mediator, you might find yourself both humble and proud. Respect for the field of mediation creates an awareness of the long line of previous contributions, putting your own contributions into perspective. But aren't you also aware of the role that luck plays in your own achievement? You know that the parties have to be *ready* to reconcile for mediation to be "successful." Yet you optimistically assume that conflicts *can* be resolved. I know that if I didn't, I wouldn't even try. You assume that not only can a conflict be resolved, but that *you* can help resolve it. But, because you know that resolution depends on the parties' willingness to reconcile, "you don't take the credit, you don't take the blame."

Finally, you feel the quiet satisfaction of knowing your presence facilitated any reconciliation that did occur.

> To suspend judgment and explore face and heart values in settings of conflict requires a capacity to develop and live with a high degree of ambiguity. On the one hand, we must accept the realness of appearance, the way things appear to be. We must on the other hand explore the realness of lived experience, how perceptions and meanings have emerged and how they might point to realities of both what is now apparent and the invisible that lies beyond what is presented as conclusive. To suspend judgment is not to relinquish opinion or the capacity to assess. It is fundamentally a force to mobilize the imagination and lift the relationship and understanding of relationships ... to a new level.
>
> John Paul Lederach,
> *The Moral Imagination*, p. 42.

7. Psychological Androgyny

Creative individuals seem to escape rigid gender role stereotyping. They are more likely to have the strengths of both. Psychological androgyny describes the ability to shift back and forth from being accommodating to assertive; facilitating the needs of the parties while protecting the integrity of the process. When tests of masculinity/femininity are given to young people, researchers find that creative and talented girls are more dominant and tougher than other girls, while creative boys are more sensitive and less aggressive than their male peers. You simultaneously have the ability to be aggressive *and* nurturing, sensitive *and* rigid, dominant *and* submissive. As a psychologically androgynous mediator, your repertoire of available responses is doubled, allowing you to interact with both parties with a far richer and varied spectrum of strengths, talents, perceptions and behaviors. (More on this in Chapter Nine: Mediation as Improvisation.)

8. Independent and Traditional

Generally, creative people are thought to be rebellious and independent. Yet to be creative within a domain you must first internalize the rules of your chosen domain: cooking, sculpture, business, teaching, or mediation. Creatives believe so completely in the importance of their chosen field that they have the discipline and persistence to learn its rules. Therefore, they are traditional even as they are independent; they stay inside the box long enough to know how the box is made before breaking outside of it. (Newbies, are you listening?) Ultimately they are willing to take the risk to break those rules and even abandon that tradition. Like Picasso.

9. Attached and Detached

Creative persons are very passionate about their profession, yet they also can be extremely objective about it. The synergistic energy generated by this tension of attachment and detachment is an important part of the mediator's work. Without passion, you can feel defeated while attempting to help the parties reconcile. Without detachment, you can lose your impartiality. After most sessions, mediators seldom find out the long term outcome of the parties' efforts. The parties may leave unresolved, to later settle or reconcile their differences. Or they may undo their agreement

... moral imagination rises with the capacity to imagine ourselves in relationship, the willingness to embrace complexity without reliance on dualistic polarity, the belief in the creative act, and acceptance of the inherent risk required to break violence and to venture on unknown paths that build constructive change.

> John Paul Lederach,
> *The Moral Imagination*, p. 29.

after the fact, based on some new slight or deliberate breach of their agreement. You seldom know what happens after the mediation ends, yet you understand and live with that reality.

10. **Openness and Vulnerability**

As the mediator, listening to parties as they speak of difficult dilemmas, it is necessary to be both open and vulnerable. The same openness and sensitivity that brings enjoyment often exposes creative mediators to a certain amount of suffering. For example, it is often financially unrewarding to be involved in such a relatively obscure, often unpaid, vocation. Nevertheless, when you are working in your area of expertise, external worries and cares fall away, replaced by a sense of contentment. This pairing of traits is why it is such a relief for me to be in the association of other mediators; to be among those I don't have to explain myself to.

BEING IN "FLOW"

"Want to have some fun?" was friend Julien Minard's first question when she called from the neighborhood program to ask my availability to mediate. She knew, without reading Maslow or Csikszentmihalyi, that creative people consistently report that they love what they do and are driven by the opportunity to do work that they enjoy doing, rather than being driven by the hope of achieving fame or fortune. I think of us as mediation junkies, always looking for our next fix.

Csikszentmihalyi was describing just that when he coined the term "flow," the quality of the experience of being involved in our chosen activity.[24] When you are in the state of flow there are clear goals every step of the way. There is a balance between challenges and skills. Action and awareness are merged while distractions are excluded from consciousness. Self-consciousness disappears so you do not worry about failure. Even the sense of time becomes distorted as the activity becomes an end in itself.

"Flow," or optimal experience, happens when the challenge is high and your skills are up to the challenge. During a flow experience, events occur in an almost automatic, effortless way. You remain in a highly focused state of consciousness while facing a clear set of goals that require immediate and appropriate responses. You become deeply involved in a self-contained

> We suggest that the most subtle influences of the mediator's affect and manner may be powerful influences in helping the mediator bring peace into the room. If this is true, then the development of our personal qualities becomes quite important. We suggest that "integration"—a quality of being in which the individual feels fully in touch with, and able to marshal, his or her mental, spiritual, and physical resources—is a way to describe what underlies presence.
>
> Daniel Bowling & David Hoffman,
> *Bringing Peace into the Room*, p. 6.

universe, unaware of time or effort, apart from ordinary life. The flow experience might be when your brain's alpha and beta waves are perfectly synchronized. They certainly provide opportunities for you to increase your positivity. Perhaps these are the times when you are fully self-actualized.

Mediation clearly offers the opportunity for these flow experiences: there are clear goals, grounded in mediation process and in your own intention. You certainly receive immediate verbal and non-verbal feedback from the parties on everything you do or say. You become transparent, lose your self-consciousness, and yet are fully present as you balance the challenge with your skills, actions and awareness. You are not distracted from the task at hand, even by a fear of failure. Time is suspended. The mediation process becomes an end in and of itself. This is "... the perfect golden moment when substance, process, and relationships come together in sync...."[25]

Think back to some of your most satisfying mediations. Did you stay motivated by the feeling of "flow," even though you sometimes experienced these sessions as painful, risky, and difficult enough to stretch your capacity? (I can think of any number of mediations that fit this description.) Yet didn't you love the creative tension? You were probably in flow; unaware of time, surfing the edge between certainty and chaos. The goals and rules for mediation created a self-contained universe where you could act without questioning what should be done next.[26]

You probably did not feel "happy" during the mediation flow experience. To experience happiness, you would have had to redirect your focus to your inner state, which would have distracted from the mediation at hand. But afterwards, reflecting on what happened, did you occasionally do your Damn-I'm-Good dance? The happiness, the positivity that follows optimal experiences leads to increasing complexity and growth in consciousness. Each mediation becomes practice for the next one. Your flow experience, your fix, becomes a magnet for learning, the opportunity to discover new things. You become continually motivated to improve your mediation skills, to keep them in balance with the challenge of future mediations. That is a measure of your increasing level of creativity.

> Mediation is not for the fainthearted; to become good at it requires facing our demons and faults, while building on our strengths.
>
> Daniel Bowling & David Hoffman,
> *Bringing Peace into the Room*, p. 4.

CHAPTER THREE

Barriers to Creative Thinking

"You're so artistic you make me sick!"

Have you ever heard that sort of dismissive response to your abilities? At the beginning of each of my creativity seminars and trainings I ask for a show of hands of those who consider themselves creative. There are a variety of responses, usually accompanied by awkward laughter. Very few confidently raise their hands high. If you are among this minority, I salute you!

Some manage an ah-shucks-I-was-taught-not-to-brag kind of embarrassed wave. Some tentatively put up their arm but keep their elbow planted at their side. Too many do not realize the extent of their creativity, or they may acknowledge it to themselves but have learned that to publically acknowledge it can leave them open to ridicule.

Are you among those reluctant to admit or even acknowledge that you are creative? What's *that* about? Does it sound too arrogant or presumptuous? Are you afraid that others will think you are a little bit nuts? Do you fear that you will be admonished, marginalized, or isolated? Negativity from others does constrict creativity. That happened to me during my introductory Creative Problem Solving course. We were all asked to brainstorm a list of ideas about some specific topic. When another student saw that my list was longer than everyone else's, she immediately declared me a "cheater!"

Who comes to mind when you think of a "creative" person? When I ask this question people generally name those with "Big C," genius levels of creativity. Did your Reticular Activating System generate the usual suspects—da Vinci, Michelangelo, Beethoven, Picasso, or Chopin? All of whom are dead, white, European males. That pretty much leaves out the rest of us; those who are living, non-Anglo, or female. Only in rare instances does

Everyone
is
just
about
as
creative
as
they
think
they
are.

someone add Bill Gates, Whoopee Goldberg, or "my sister."

We have been programmed to believe the long-standing fallacy that *all* creativity is "Big C" creativity—a mystery, a rare form of genius, possessed by only a few with special talents or wildly innovative ideas. Here in *Picasso* I am talking about "little c" creativity, the kind you use every day to solve everyday problems. The kind you use when you are mediating, when you are in flow, enjoying those moments of self-actualization. The kind you encourage in your clients.

When you were younger did you think you were creative? I certainly didn't grow up thinking so. The Picasso family's values of encouraging children were not known at my house. Quite the contrary, I was not allowed to continue anything I excelled at. Think about that. Trapped in a double bind, I could only pursue things in which I was either mediocre or disinterested. When I was four, Mom even told the neighbors to discourage my "precociousness" or I would become a "brat." In response, my favorite neighbor, Chuck, called me "Brat" as a term of endearment. When I was little he was the only one I remember ever encouraging me. Then Chuck died. His death entrenched in my young mind the futility of striving for anything because I would lose it anyway.

As a fourth grader I was invited to be part of both the Special Art and Special Music programs. My mother told me I could only be in one, and decided it should be Special Music Chorus, even though I could not read music or distinguish proper pitch. The art teacher, who knew my mother, eventually asked me why I wasn't in Special Art. When I relayed my mother's decision, the art teacher replied with a clenched jaw, "You could have been in both."

It took me years to claim my creative potential. What's stopping *you* from claiming yours? What aspects of your belief system prevent you from being a more fully creative person? Answers to these questions usually point to early personal, perceptual or cultural blocks. Further, these beliefs are usually self-imposed and/or unconscious—a bad combination. But they can dissolve when exposed to new information. You have watched as mediation parties' eyes widen in the sudden recognition of a new aspect of a situation. The same is true for you.

"House" in Hindi and English

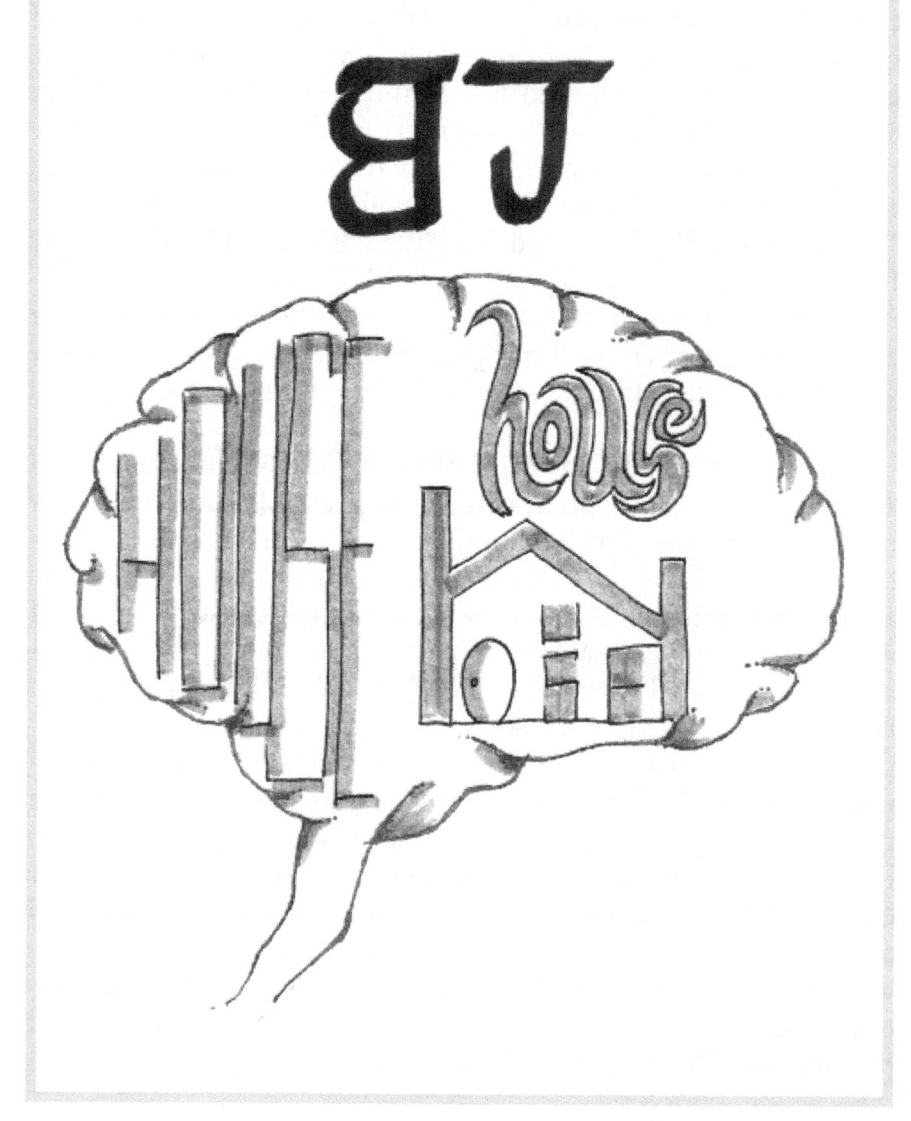

What were *you* told at an early age? That the tree you drew wasn't good enough? That your purple hand print did not look uniform enough to hang in the hall with the rest of the students' pictures? To stay inside the lines?

Creativity workshop participants routinely tell horror stories of ways in which their creativity was stifled. One remembered that he could not read standard music notation in his middle school orchestra class. As a result, he laboriously transcribed the regular music notes into his own musical language. One day his music teacher saw his translation, grabbed the boy by the shoulder and demanded to know what he thought he was doing! The boy was kicked out of class, failed the course, and never played his clarinet again.

Another participant remembered his photography instructor telling him, with finality, that he just did not understand perspective. The teacher quit trying to teach him. Instead he just wrote him off as incapable of learning.

The students' recollections are always quite vivid. Here is why. Your brain remembers all sorts of information, especially memories with an emotional charge, by making associations and links.[1] Remember, your Reticular Activating System (RAS), your brain's editor, controls the brain wave activity linked to your subconscious mind. The brain has the tremendous ability to store information and remember it when the right association is triggered, often through figurative language and metaphor. Which is why I learned early on to associate "having" with "losing." The resulting message was "Sigh—no point in even trying." (More on metaphors in Chapter Seven.)

One writer uses a meat grinder metaphor to describe another aspect of scotomas, those mental blind spots. As new information gets fed through the meat grinder of your narrative, contradictory facts get pulverized like gristle, and you are left with a 'truth' that validates only what you believed all along. Superimposing a favorite narrative over an incident can make you miss things you otherwise might have seen. "Is it fact, or just a narrative squeezed through the meat grinder? Truth, or just its emotional equivalent?"[2]

The good news is that your RAS also allows you to recognize patterns and symbols, not just negative childhood memories. Look at the images on the left. The top one is unfamiliar, yet

> ... few mediators take the time to ... identify the thoughts, beliefs, values, and principles that are the foundation for the way they experience and understand behavior, events, and interactions. Failure to do so can lead to blind spots, which limit mediators' ability to understand, interpret, and act integratively.
>
> Michael D. Lang & Alison Taylor,
> *The Making of a Mediator*, p. 94.

you immediately recognize the bottom images as variations on the word "house." That is your RAS at work, relying on pattern memory, aka snowflakes. This ability also helps you recall more trivial things that have been stored away for years, like jokes ("So, this duck walks into a bar…") and song lyrics ("I can't get no…"). It also recalls relevant stories that can leapfrog scotomas, removing that block to your creativity. The more you store information in patterns that have strong associations, the more you develop your brain's untapped abilities to remember, recall, learn, combine and recombine, and thus be more creative.[3] Keep pattern memory in mind as you read on. One exercise in the *Picasso Workbook* provides the opportunity to think of interesting, unusual, and complete pictures you can draw from circles on the page. What was your first reaction to those directions? What scotoma became a firewall? The perennial favorite response is, "I can't draw!"

People are often reluctant to risk exposing their self-imposed lack of visual creativity. They recall a grade school incident that destroyed their creativity on the spot. For example, a sixty-something creativity class student was convinced that she could not draw. She balked at even attempting some simple line drawings for an in-class assignment. When she upended her mental Snow Globe to rummage around old traumas on the subject, she suddenly remembered the origin of her unconscious scotoma. She had gotten a D in her third grade art class! (If that teacher is still alive she should be flogged.)

I modified the assignment to encourage her to make some sketches. Having released her scotoma, her first drawing was a recognizable sketch of her husband, including his beard and glasses. By the end of the term she and her husband were making plans to turn an extra bedroom into her art studio.

My own personal performance scotoma is not visual, it's auditory. While in the fourth grade, not able to read music or hear proper pitch, I was forced to take piano lessons. To my relief, within months of beginning the lessons, my piano teacher told my parents that they were wasting their money.

Fast forward to my college elementary education music class. The course required all of us to teach a short song to the class. The assignment was to sing a line of the song, have the class repeat the line, then sing the next one, and so on. Now, I have a good voice, but apparently I really cannot distinguish between

> Finding positive meaning is always possible.... to find the good and honestly accentuate the positive meaning in your current circumstances is always present, even if it's simply to realize that "this too shall pass."
>
> Barbara Fredrickson, *Positivity*, p. 182.

keys. When it was my turn, I sang a line, they repeated the line. Each time I sang the next line, I unknowingly changed to a different key. People snickered as I naively struggled on to the end. Finally, my instructor raised his head from his hands and, with a sigh, recommended I buy a pitch pipe. That ended my singing career. To this day I will not sing where anyone can hear me. It's my scotoma and I'm sticking to it.

NEGATIVITY

Positivity is essential to everyone's growth and well being. It broadens your mind and expands your range of vision. But its effect is only temporary. Negativity is its flipside. It narrows your mind and contracts your range of vision. Your mind experiences moments of expanded and retracted awareness as positivity and negativity flow through you.[4] The most common forms of negativity—anger, shame, contempt, disgust, embarrassment, guilt, hate, sadness, fear, and stress—constrict your thinking and creativity.

For people to flourish there needs to be a positivity/negativity ratio of at least three to one. This means that for every negative emotional experience you endure, you need to experience at least three positive emotional experiences that uplift you. Three to one is the ratio that research found to be the tipping point, predicting whether people languish or flourish.

The 3:1 ratio was determined as the result of studying the characteristics of high-performance business teams.[5] They were observed as they met in board rooms equipped with one way mirrors. During hour-long business meetings everything the teams said was recorded and coded. Three dimensions were tracked: whether people's statements were 1) positive or negative, 2) self-focused or other focused, 3) based on inquiry (asking questions) or advocacy (defending a point of view). The researchers also measured a variable called connectivity, a reflection of how attuned or responsive team members were to one another and how much each team member influenced the behavior of others.

Not surprisingly, those classified as the highest performing teams (in terms of profit and customer satisfaction, among other things), had an unusually high, 6:1, positivity to negativity ratio.

Teams with mixed performance, only a ratio of 2:1, lacked resiliency. They got stuck in negative, self-absorbed advocacy. Their

Words That Reflect Negativity

afraid	ashamed	blameworthy
blushing	contemptuous	disgraced
disdainful	distrust	downhearted
embarrassed	fearful	guilty
hate	humiliated	irritated
nervous	overwhelmed	repentant
sad	scared	scornful
self-conscious	stressed	unhappy

Barbara Fredrickson, *Positivity*, pp. 142-143.

extreme negativity caused these teams to lose their flexibility and ability to objectively question others. They no longer listened to each other. They just waited to speak and defend their own views. Each person was critical of everyone else. They languished in an endless loop of negativity. Those teams sound much like many intact work groups I have facilitated and mediated. And they were not even the worst teams in the study.

The lowest performing teams had a positivity/negativity ratio of only 1:1. They were entrenched in negative and self-absorbed advocacy. They simply defended their own views while being highly critical of everyone else. They had almost no tendency to question or focus outward. They spiraled down to a stalemate.

It is important to note that that the prescription for positivity is not 3:0. Negativity is still important. Even the happiest people cry when they lose someone they love. According to Fredrickson, they are "angered by injustice and frightened by danger. Their stomachs turn when they see vomit or witness human atrocities. The beauty of the 3-to-1 ratio is that it's large enough to encompass the full range of human emotions. There are no emotions that need to be forever shunned or suppressed."[6] Negativity just needs to be balanced with enough positivity to allow the person to still thrive. As mediators we provide that balance for the parties, for at least the duration of the mediation session.

Researcher and author John Gottman[7] has done extensive work on the impact of negativity. He concludes that there is such a thing as appropriate negativity. According to Gottman, anger and engagement in conflict can be healthy and productive forms of negativity, whereas expressions of disgust and contempt are more corrosive. The difference has to do with where the negativity is focused. Guilt results from seeing something you did as wrong or immoral. You can resolve it by making amends and find a better way to behave. Shame, on the other hand, is not just that you did something wrong, it implies you yourself are wrong or immoral. Both "contempt and shame ... are all encompassing and difficult to overcome."[8] Consider how a positivity to negativity ratio of 3:1 factors into your life as you continue reading about blocks and barriers to your inherent creativity. You can go online to www.PositivityRatio.com to track your positivity over time.

Johari Window

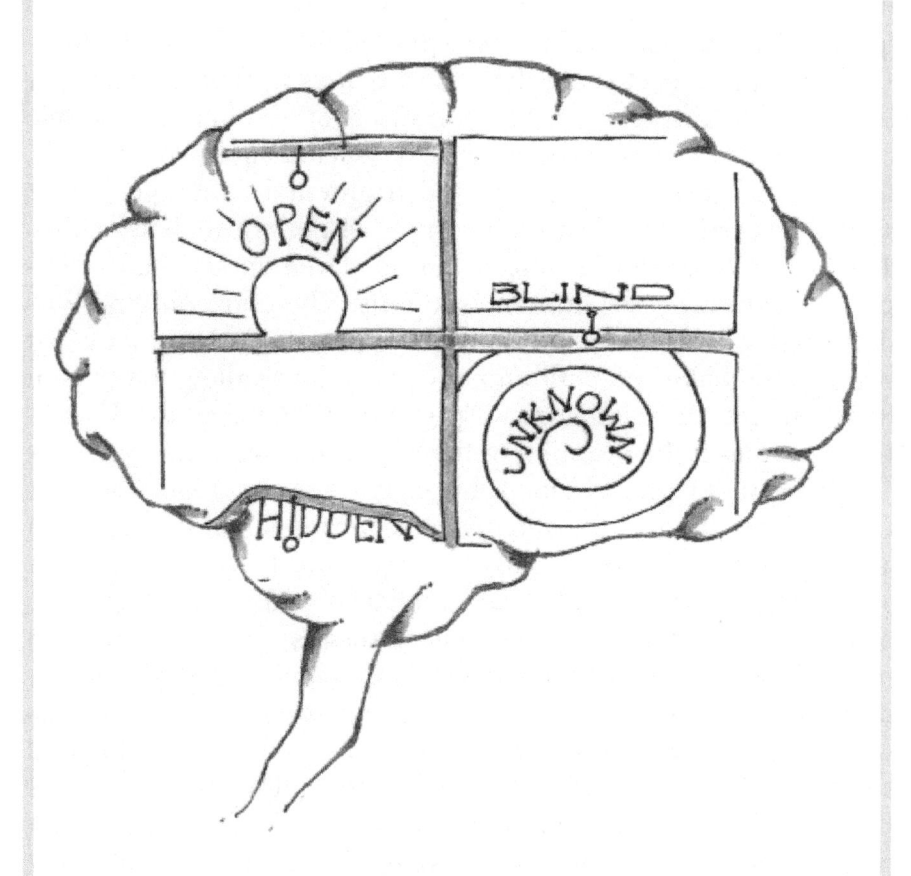

Anita Kelly & Kevin McKillop,
Consequences of Revealing Personal Secrets, p. 450.

THE JOHARI WINDOW

The Johari Window[9] is a metaphorical description of how mental blocks operate, for the parties in your mediations as well as for you. It's a useful model for increasing the kind of self-understanding and self-awareness that can overcome blocks to your creativity. As you see on the facing page, a four-pane window divides your personal awareness into different kinds as represented by its quadrants: Open, Hidden, Blind, and Unknown. The lines dividing the four panes are like window shades, which move as information is brought to consciousness. The goal is to reduce the other areas, enlarging your Open Area and increasing your positivity and self-actualization.

Open Area

The Open Area is easy. It is that part of your aware, conscious and revealed self that is also known to others: physical attributes, stated attitudes, visible behavior, and apparent motivations. It includes those parts of your creativity that you readily acknowledge. You're an open book. Anyone who has not met me can spot me drinking tea at Starbucks: the cheerful short, white, past middle-aged bespectacled female with short gray hair and sturdy shoes.

Unknown Area

At the other extreme, the Unknown Area of the window encompasses those rich and complex areas of your unconscious that no one is unaware of. The Unknown Area holds deeply engrained unconscious blocks, making them difficult to overcome because you don't even know they are there. Yet from time to time something happens, you intuitively feel, read, hear, or dream, and something from your unconscious is revealed. "Aha! My art teacher!" Pay attention to your pattern memories as you read *Picasso*. Reading the saga of *my* unconscious mental barriers and my efforts to uncover and resolve them may prompt you to recall *your* own old pattern memories that remain unresolved blocks.

Looking back, I am amazed at all the self-imposed blocks that stood in my way of writing this book. After graduate school I worked more than full time. While heading the Alternative Dispute Resolution department at the Better Business Bureau I started teaching a creativity class at Marylhurst University. I also began a consulting practice, mediating and presenting workshops on creativity and conflict resolution.

> Creativity—bringing something new into being—involves releasing the old, whether the old is an idea, an assumption, a value, or a way of ordering life.
>
> Michelle LeBaron,
> *Bridging Troubled Waters*, p. 36.

Way back then I thought to myself, "I should write a book about all this." Although conceptually it was still a mediation book, the outline seemed very clear to me. So I got a three-ring binder, labeled the tabs, and filled it with handouts. But, of course, I got busy with other things and the notebook languished on a shelf. Time went by. Again I thought to myself, "I should write a book on the connections between creativity and conflict resolution." Again I got a three-ring binder, labeled some tabs, and filled it with even more handouts from both disciplines. All I had to do, I thought to myself, was to create a narrative that allowed others to make the same obvious connections that I had made. But again, life got in the way. I was somehow stuck at that early phase of the project. That notebook also sat on the shelf.

At the meta level, creative thinking can be limited by cultural boundaries such as traditions, customs, rules, regulations, procedures, social norms and influences. They are not automatically bad; we need some agreements, like traffic lights, to function in society. Cultural blocks are only problematic when they are part of your Unknown Area. Then these unconscious barriers can prevent even the consideration of new ideas or approaches to conflict. Like my early childhood assumption, "I can't have it, there's no point asking."

Hidden Area

The content of the Hidden Area of your Johari Window is not known to others unless you choose to disclose it. It contains those things you are modest about as well as ashamed of, including self judgments ("I'm not creative."), imagined shortcomings, or fantasies, which you don't share out of fear of rejection. The degree to which you expand your Open Area depends on your willingness to risk disclosing private details about yourself.

For years, the biggest secret in my Hidden Area was having been adopted, something shameful in 1950s American culture. While growing up I shared this dark secret with only a few trusted friends. Words like "misbegotten" and "ill-conceived" were not lost on me. Even as a kid I noted that one of the worst things you can call someone is a "bastard." You can bet I guarded that part of my Hidden Area.

Meanwhile, the book idea drifted to the background, behind consulting projects, contract mediations, and teaching. Years

Perceptual Blocks to Creative Thinking

Habits that distract from or prevent creative/critical thinking

- Assuming information is accurate or complete
- Jumping to conclusions
- A negative attitude toward creative thinking
- Resisting new ideas that might be presented
- Remaining unaware of new meanings, relationships or applications
- Feeling isolated

> Gary Davis, *Creativity is Forever*, pp. 8-10.

went by. After I remarried, my husband and I built a house together. When I moved my office into the new house I found a *third* three-ring binder filled with handouts! I was stunned; I had no memory of even compiling it.

But by then I had learned to ask the voice in my left ear, "What's *this* all about?" (That is the same voice that previously had advised me to "Get a dog." and admonished me that "This will be your last cup of coffee.") After a pause, the response that came back was, "If you write this book, your mother will ridicule you." "Wow," I chuckled back to my voice, "Mom's been dead for five years now; do you think it's safe?!" Talk about an unconscious, completely self-imposed personal block! Talk about negativity!

Blind Area
Your Blind Area holds your emotional and perceptual barriers to creative thinking.[10] Perceptual blocks lurk in the Blind Area as scotomas, those entrenched mental habits, meat grinder truths, paradigms and mental models that distract from or prevent your creative thinking. Scotomas filter information contrary to what you believe to be true. Especially what you *know* to be true! Contrary messages get blocked out and never reach your cerebrum to even become thoughts and/or emotions.

When the parties operate out of their Blind Area they both jump to their own meat grinder conclusions, especially if one of the conclusions is that they already have all the information they need. Think of the times during mediation when you have watched a disputant, with little information about the actions or beliefs of the other party, know how and why they themselves would act in the same circumstances. They immediately project that same intent across the table. Yet, the other party may have had a very different, more productive or even helpful intent. Over the years I have learned that during those difficult mediations I can help the parties gain access to those parts of their brain that allow their own creativity to shine through their mental barriers and scotomas. As the mediator, you are doing the same thing as you probe both their assumptions and intentions, and let them surprise themselves and each other.

Case in point: The woman before me in the mediation looked completely beaten. In her life experience as a Native American, she knew all too well the futility of going against the three white

Cultural Blocks to Creative Thinking

Boundaries that distract from or prevent creative/critical thinking

- Conforming to established:
    - traditions and customs
    - rules, regulations and procedures
    - social norms and influences
- Reliance on technology
- Dependence on experts
- Over-emphasis on competition or cooperation

Gary Davis, *Creativity is Forever*, pp. 8-10.

males across the table. Plus she was in a bureaucratic double-bind: She was being evicted because her children had been taken away; without her children, she could not stay in her low income, government-controlled housing. But she couldn't get her children back without a place to live.

When I asked her what she wanted from the mediation, all she could whisper was, "I don't know, whatever they want." I finally leaned down very close to her and whispered back, "If you *did* know what you want, what would that be?" She sat up slightly and responded, "To get my children back."

Up until then she had not been able to bypass her scotoma's Blind Area and articulate her needs. The landlord finally knew what she wanted from the mediation. The mood of the mediation shifted as the landlord and his agents began explaining what steps she could take to get custody of her children while keeping her housing. Suddenly, the gridlocked conflict had the potential for resolution.

By shifting the question from real to hypothetical, I helped the mother gain access to a part of her brain not blocked by her current, negative reality. The causes of her conflict were perceptual, personal *and* cultural. She was overwhelmed with regret from having lost her children while being forced to navigate the white man's legal system.

In another case, the teen in the landlord/tenant eviction mediation did not look much like a gang member, slouched there with his headset draped around the collar of his Hawaiian shirt. Nevertheless, that was the manager's meat grinder assumption and the reason for the eviction. The young man was on the police's gang registry. Of *course* he was in a gang. He and his single mom had to go. End of discussion.

I asked the teen, "What would have caused the police to put your name on the gang registry?" He told the story of how he and his middle school buddies used to hang out at the local convenience store, being annoying enough for the police to take down their names. He had long ago parted company with those boys, who did go on to join a gang. But his name remained on the registry. Further questioning revealed that his goal was to graduate from high school and join the Coast Guard. Asked why he wanted to join the Coast Guard, he said, "To earn money for college so I can join the police force."

Discomfort is the nerve ending of growth.

Jonathan Rowe,
From Raising Hell to Raising Barns

The manager's jaw dropped. Aha! This kid was a far cry from what he had assumed! The manager's Blind Area line shifted toward Open. Rather than continue with the eviction discussion, the manager immediately began offering him advice on how to get off the gang registry.

Your Blind Area also includes personality traits, habits and mannerisms, as well as your creativity, which you don't see about yourself, but others see in you. By asking for feedback as well as disclosing private information, you further increase the size of your Open Area, expanding the reality of who you are.

Meanwhile, back to writing *Picasso*. I soon found that overcoming my fear of my deceased adoptive mother's scorn was only my first step. My next barrier was easier to uncover; my fear that the mediation community would ridicule me. To overcome that block I put together 25 tentative pages; a bunch of the handouts put into the same font and strung together with minimum narrative. Then, with great fear and trepidation, I asked a select group of trusted mediator friends to read them and give me feedback. Wow! No one ridiculed me!

It was about this time I had yet another Blinding Flash of the Obvious. My book did not even have to be a *mediation* book. It could be a *creative* book about mediation! Wow squared! I was off! All my blocks overcome … or so I thought.

After receiving positive feedback from my mediator buddies, I went on to draft a substantial manuscript. But wait. The next hurtle was the legal mediation community. Certainly they would ridicule me. So I gave a draft to a couple of lawyer/mediator friends to critique. They were also supportive. So far, so good.

One, Sam Imperati, spent a very valuable two hours (valuable to me, frustrating for him) critiquing *Picasso*. He had a particular concern with one section and recommended substantial changes. My response was that the creativity researcher involved would not only ridicule me but certainly would sue me if I challenged his work. To which Sam responded, "Fuck him." That exchange jarred open yet one more scotoma. I realized with a shock that I still feared yet another group—the creativity community. Thanks, Sam, I needed that!

Again, I deliberately set out to overcome the creative block *du jour* by presenting a Mediating with Picasso workshop at the 2006 Creative Problem Solving Institute in Chicago. In 2008,

> If we sense some incompleteness or disharmony, tension is aroused. We are uncomfortable and want to relieve the tension.
>
> E. Paul Torrance,
> *Scientific Views of Creativity and Factors Affecting Its Growth*, p. 217.

I presented a workshop at the 2008 Creativity and Innovation Management Conference. Responses were overwhelmingly favorable. All their questions centered on how to manage conflict in *their* Creative Problem Solving sessions. Ta da! The final hurdle.

One way to raise your awareness about your own Hidden and Blind blocks and increase your Open Area is to consider what behaviors were not allowed when you were growing up. What belief systems were normal when you were very young, before you were aware enough to question them? What seemed normal to you then may have become creative blocks entrenched in your unconscious today.

Take the example of Alicia, who complained in mediation that her neighbor's dog, Buffy, barked at her whenever she was in her own driveway, which was situated close to Buffy's kennel. Alicia had been afraid of dogs ever since she'd been bitten as a child. Both her Hidden and Blind Areas were convinced that Buffy was just as vicious. Yet she also had concerns for her safety while jogging. Meanwhile, Buffy was home alone all day, bored and just looking for action. By the end of the mediation Alicia agreed to meet Buffy and finally attempt to overcome her childhood fear of dogs. It occurred to Alicia that if she got over her fear of Buffy they could exercise together. Win/win. Alicia and Buffy out jogging together, who would have thought?

Some childhood beliefs are of no consequence. I was told as a child that eating cookie dough would give me worms. That belief remained, unchallenged, into adulthood until my scientifically-minded daughter asked me, "And where would the worms come from, Mom?" For the first time in my life I thought through the absurdity of the belief, and sheepishly replied, "Oh ... well, never mind." Are you remembering some of your childhood beliefs?

Some Blind Area beliefs form blocks that are so deeply engrained that they take years to overcome. One of mine lasted until I was 43, sitting in a Portland State University career counselor's office trying to decide what to do when I grew up. She said, "It sounds like you need an advanced degree in order to legitimize yourself." I burst into tears, denying I had said anything like that. She assured me that "legitimate" was indeed the word I had used. I suddenly realized that all those years I had believed I could not excel in life because I had been illegitimate! "Is that all?!" I responded. A month later I was in Buffalo applying to

Personal Blocks to Creative Thinking

Emotions that distract from or prevent creative/critical thinking
- Fear:
    - failure or success
    - rejection or ridicule
    - supervisors or subordinates
- Anger
- Emotional numbness
- Anxiety
- Lack of self-confidence
- Stress
- Excess enthusiasm
- Poor health

Gary Davis, *Creativity is Forever*, pp. 8-10.

graduate school.

What deep seated negative beliefs are you carrying around? Overcoming limiting beliefs can seem like peeling away never-ending layers of onion. This came solidly home to me during my first solo mediation. As Martha relentlessly harangued and nagged her neighbor, Jessie, about her dog. I sat silently by, like a doe in the headlights, helpless to intervene. Fortunately, my coach, Jamie Damon, finally called for a private meeting with me and all but threw cold water in my face to get me to snap to. "Why are you letting Martha go on like that?"

The problem was that Martha reminded me of my mother and I unconsciously believed that if I challenged her I would die. That was *me* in Jessie's chair. I was stuck in the past, being berated one more time. After that early mediation I knew that I needed to take positive action. Through some neurology-based alternative therapy sessions I deleted the unconscious childhood belief that it was far too dangerous for me to challenge my mother's anger. Because I wanted to become a competent mediator, I had to learn to be in the "here and now," not held back by my old, Blind Area fears; old barriers to my creativity.

My family-of-origin blocks produced a voice of judgment that continued to ridicule me during most of my early mediations. That old voice in my left ear said, "You're in over your head. You don't know what you are doing." That pesky voice only lasted an instant before I could refocus my attention on the parties. I learned to expect it, even greet it—"You again?" and humor it—"Anything else?" before it finally retreated. That voice still pipes up from time to time, like an annoying old jingle I hoped I'd never hear again.

If you recognize yourself in the above story, or recall a similar one, various kinds of personal work can help you overcome the cultural, personal and/or perceptual blocks that prevent you from mediating with a Picasso mind.

The fact is, every time you solve a problem, step out of your routine, and make unique connections, you are being creative. You are creating new connections in *your* brain, even if someone else has already made those connections. When you are making them, you are being creative. Again, everyone is creative, albeit with differing creative strengths. And, everyone is just about as creative as they think they are.

If the prospect of taking some chances and going through a difficult period of transition seems daunting, it should also seem familiar; it is what we ask our clients to do every time they participate in a significant resolution effort. And as the notion that the first step in change is to question the beliefs that we rely on and often comfort us, that too should not seem so unusual, because that is also the largest challenge people face in altering their approach to conflict.

Bernard Mayer, *Beyond Neutrality*, p. 78.

Finally, another block to your own creative thinking can be subscribing too completely to a single prevailing mediation philosophy. What limiting personal, perceptual or culture beliefs about the field of mediation prevent you from becoming a more creative mediator? What scotomas have you already encountered reading this book? Where does your resistance come from? What information given here has run counter to how you were initially trained as a mediator?

How might you reframe those blocks in ways that allow your Reticular Activating System to let the information *in* rather than causing your scotomas to keep it *out*? In what ways might this expand your Open Area?

> Intuition appears magical, out of the mediator's control, and truly alarming. In fact, what passes for intuition is a form of artistry ... (which) can be defined, understood, and learned, especially as mediators reflect on their constellation of theories that guide them.
>
> Michael D. Lang & Alison Taylor,
> *The Making of a Mediator*, p. 112.

Historical Attitudes Toward Creativity

"Relax, it may be only mental illness."

Woody Allen's comment is a fit response to the still-evolving definitions and assumptions about creativity. These definitions have historically made it alright for someone to be *sort of* creative, but it was definitely not safe to be *too* creative. Being called "creative" still carries the connotation that there just might be something wrong with you, an accusation of some kind of defect. Here is why.

For most of human history "creation" was believed to be the sole prerogative of supreme beings. Only since recorded histories have we seen evidence that cultures expanded their view of creativity to see it as a human trait.[1] It was not until long after written language was invented that evidence can be cited for the awareness of the "unconscious." In 1976 psychologist Julian Jaynes proposed a fascinating theory that until only recently in recorded history (900 BC), humans had bicameral, or divided, minds.[2] He maintained that before that time the two sides of the human brain did not communicate with each other. Instead, intuitive thinking was attributed to an outside source. The gods spoke to individuals and directed their behavior. Today it would be like believing that a god drove your car down the freeway while you carried on a conversation with your passenger.

Later, ancient Greeks initiated the "which-came-first-the-chicken-or-egg?" debate over creativity's origins. Plato maintained that the source of creativity was "undetermined," independent of natural and human resources. It was the work of the Muse, their divine source of inspiration. Plato argued that the creative person was "out of his mind" during the creative process. This correlates to Jaynes' bicameral theory. Plato's early thinking became the basis for the traditional Western interpretation that the creative

Creativity Misconceptions Debunked

Creativity is NOT ...
> a vague, amorphous, overused buzz word.
>
> spontaneous and undisciplined.
>
> only among a chosen few.
>
> woo-woo, magic or trickery.
>
> mostly about product innovation.

Creativity does NOT mean detachment from the real world.

You do NOT have to be a little bit nuts to be creative.

> Donald Treffinger, Scott Isaksen, & Brian Dorval, *Creative Problem Solving: An Introduction*, pp. 3-4.

process involved mystery, insanity, or altered states of consciousness.[3]

Later, Aristotle, a more rationalist thinker, initiated the "determinist" view that the creative process obeyed natural laws. Aristotle logically argued that it was not possible for anything to be produced out of nothing. Obviously and necessarily, some part of the resulting creative product had to have previously existed. Aristotle's creativity (the egg?) is from an identifiable source, an adaptation of something already in existence (the chicken?). The iPod is an example of a combination of existing concepts: microcomputer technology, earphones, and recorded music.

The apparent paradox is that creativity has both determined and undetermined aspects. Both chicken and egg. Creations must simultaneously be recognizable and familiar enough to be identified as new, yet radical and unfamiliar.

Plato's "undetermined" creative products are rarer. They represent totally new innovations: heavier-than-air flight, the telephone, and microchips. The creator's intuitive leaps are much more difficult to explain. This is why innovative "undetermined" creative people often have been discriminated against, even as their products change the way we live.

Fast forward from Aristotle and Plato's time to the eighteenth century. Impressed by Darwin's theory of evolution, his cousin, Francis Galton, attempted to explain how human faculties, including creativity, were transmitted generation to generation by correlating genius with hereditary factors.[4] Through extensive "research" on notable British men he proved that being born into a wealthy upper class family was a reliable indicator of high creative ability.

Here is where it gets bad. In the late nineteenth century insanity referred to any deviation from ordinary or normal behavior. Cesare Lombroso,[5] an Italian psychiatrist, associated genius with insanity by distinguishing differences between talent and genius. A talented person could explain how and why he reached a given theory, a genius could not. Therefore Lombroso concluded that the conception of genius, what we would call Plato's undetermined highly innovative creative thinking, was totally involuntary. Out of control. His conclusion—highly creative people must be crazy.

Ironically, recent brain research has shown that "Big C" creatives *do* have a higher instance of mood disorders. Andreasen,

CHAPTER FOUR—HISTORICAL ATTITUDES TOWARD CREATIVITY | 89

Signs of Fatal Hereditary Degeneration

- Shortness
- Pale skin
- Prominent ears
- Irregular teeth
- A skimpy beard
- Left handedness
- Stammering
- Early sexual development
- Excessive originality
- Choosing not to marry
- Preference for travel

Creativity was synonymous with epilepsy.

> Adapted from Cesare Lombroso,
> *Genius and Insanity*, pp. 79-82.

author of *The Creating Brain*[6] reports that

> "The evidence supporting an association between artistic creativity and mood disorders is quite solid, as is the absence of an association with schizophrenia. The nature of artistic creativity, particularly literary creativity, is probably not compatible with the presence of an illness like schizophrenia, which causes many of its victims to be socially withdrawn and cognitively disorganized ..."

So relax, it may *not* be mental illness.

Meanwhile, back in the nineteenth century, Lombroso extensively documented even the physical descriptions of deviant behavior in those he considered men of genius. Building on Galton's research, Lombroso concluded that a large percentage of their mental and physical afflictions were the result of fatal hereditary degeneration and were passed on to their children.

It gets even worse. According to Lombroso, additional indicators of this fatal insane "genius" degeneration included irregular teeth, prominent ears, shortness, pale skin, a skimpy beard, left handedness, stammering, and early sexual development. Not content with those attributes, Lombroso included excessive originality, choosing not to marry, and a preference for travel. Lombroso further noted that there were more signs of degeneration in "men of genius" than in the average man. He therefore concluded that the coincidence of genius and insanity provided an understanding of "the astonishing unconsciousness, instantaneousness and intermittence of the creations of genius, hence its great resemblance to epilepsy."[7]

Lombroso's prejudicial conclusions made it downright dangerous for his contemporaries to be considered too creative, let alone to have certain "undesirable" physical characteristics that had nothing to do with mental health or creativity. He helped generate and perpetuate the continuing stigma attached to undetermined, innovative "little c" creative thinking. (More on this in Chapter Five: Styles of Creativity.)

Toward the present day, Sigmund Freud replaced Plato's Muses with the concept of the Unconscious. Later, Otto Rank deviated from mainstream psychoanalytic thought that equated artistic activity with neurosis by formulating personality differences that distinguished between the artist type, the neurotic type, and the adaptive type. Rank held that while the artist type

Attributes of Mental Health

- Mental flexibility
- Freedom to learn through experience
- Freedom to change with changing internal and external circumstances
- Ability to be influenced by reasonable argument
- Ability to appeal to emotions

> Lawrence Kubie,
> *Creation and Neurosis*, pp. 143-148.

(Plato's undetermined, innovative creativity) was an ideal to strive for, anyone with that type was inevitably in conflict with society.[8] More reasons to "act normal." It was not until 1952 that psychoanalyst Ernst Kris separated regression in the creative process from regression connected to psychotic states.[9] In other words, you don't have to be psychotic to be creative. It was not until 1958, in his work on the neurotic distortion of the creative process, that psychiatrist Lawrence Kubie held an even more positive position. He maintained that people's neuroses were based on their mental rigidity, regardless of their style or level of creativity. He concluded that a person's mental health can be measured by five attributes: mental flexibility, freedom to learn through experience, freedom to change with changing internal and external circumstances, the ability to be influenced by reasonable argument, and the person's ability to appeal to emotions.[10]

Which brings us back to Maslow's 1960's correlation between creativity and mental health. The sixty-something years of creativity research has not completely discredited a concept whose historical roots include such damaging prejudice against innocent people. Although the psychological literature has finally associated creativity with mental health and self-actualizing personal growth, sometimes it seems like the word has not yet reached the general public (although the advent of computers has ushered in the revenge of the nerds).

Unfortunately, it is normal for old stereotypes and meat grinder prejudices to prevail, even when people are presented with new evidence. Innovation diffusion theory has shown that it takes the acceptance of only 15% of any given population for an idea to be considered mainstream.[11] Handicapped access did not become the norm until wheelchair-bound Viet Nam vets came home and could not cross a city street, enter public buildings or reach public pay phones. Before that, people lacking mobility were just considered "shut-ins." Consider how long it took for people to comprehend that the world was round. Or the dangers of smoking. Or climate change. Or the value of mediation in resolving legal and other disputes.

Since the 1950s hundreds of studies have linked creativity with intelligence, invention and innovation, the study of "problem finding," the development of creative potential, the assessment of creative thinking, and the identification of a wide variety

> Creativity and courage have long been soul mates. Even at the most simple level, a new idea represents a new connection, something that hasn't been put together before. It requires the creative person to stand up and dare to be different.
>
> Daz Rudkin, Dave Allan,
> Kris Murrin, & Matt Kingdon,
> *Sticky Wisdom*, p. 167.

of intellectual attributes.[12] Research has also determined that creativity is about more than just product innovation. Creativity also involves thoughts, concepts, designs, wonderings, decisions based on new criteria, new perceptions, and new resolutions to existing problems.

In 1972 a classic study[13] found that creativity is not only spontaneous and undisciplined, it can be taught. Students who completed a two-year program in creativity and innovation performed significantly better in situational tests dealing with real-life, relevant situations than the comparable control students. "Most students reported large gains in their own productive, creative behavior, as well as their ability to cope with day-to-day problems. Their creativity couldn't help spilling over into vast areas of their lives!"[14] By the mid-1980s, while I was in graduate school, major studies in the development of creativity overwhelmingly proved that when creative abilities are nurtured, significant positive results occur.[15]

A month after my brief encounter with the PSU career counselor I was on a plane to Buffalo to check out the master's program at Buff State. That happened to be the middle weekend of an introductory course, *Nurturing Creativity*, where Creative Problem Solving (CPS) was introduced. I was allowed to fully participate, during which time I applied CPS methods and techniques to my question "Wouldn't it be nice if I could begin graduate school at the Center for Studies in Creativity?" I flew home three days later with a Plan of Action. I experienced for myself what the earlier creativity study had demonstrated; that I can be deliberately creative, even under pressure. Over the years I have found that this is true even during difficult mediations. I can help the parties gain access to those parts of their brain that allow their own creativity to shine through their mental barriers and scotomas. So can you!

What I repeatedly found was that once I cleared away my blocks to moving forward with my life, everything seemed to slide into place, and support my intent. In the three months between my March application to Buff State and my arrival to begin the program, I methodically found answers to all the challenges my departure had on the lives of seven other people. My oldest was in college. My second daughter, a high school sophomore, wanted to come with me. My youngest, in middle school, wanted to stay

Until one is committed there is hesitancy, the chance to draw back, always ineffectiveness. Concerning all acts of initiative (and creation), there is one elementary truth,... that the moment one definitely commits oneself, then Providence moves too. All sorts of things occur to help one that would never otherwise have occurred. A whole stream of events issues from the decision, raising in one's favour all manner of unforeseen incidents and meetings and material assistance, which no man could have dreamt would have come his way. I have learned a deep respect for one of Goethe's couplets:

Whatever you can do, or dream you can, begin it.
Boldness has genius, power, and magic in it.

>W.H. Murray,
>*The Scottish Himalayan Expedition*, pp. 6-7.

in her home and familiar school. So I negotiated with my former husband (plus his girl friend and her two boys) to move into my house in my absence and resume the mortgage payments. My golden retriever needed to stay at home. I gave my VISA number to the vet so my former husband could take her there without having to pay the bill. Then I methodically told the neighbors my plans and basically, what to think; "I know you'll want to welcome Tom back into the neighborhood."

Then I went back to the bank to get a second equity loan on the house (the first one financed my initial dispute resolution certificate at Willamette Law School). When the banker asked, "What would work for you?" I replied, "Free money." Her response was, "No problem; that's called an irregular amortization." She made available what I needed for the entire time I was in graduate school, but deferred the increased interest until after I returned. Worked for me!

My Shuffling Off to Buffalo story is an example of what can happen when Blind, unconscious blocks to creative thinking are finally removed. What challenges have been on *your* mind lately? What sorts of things would you like to accomplish, or at least begin this year? What's stopping you?

Style vs. Level of Creativity

Level of Creativity

Style of Creativity

The Kirton Adaption-Innovation Inventory (KAI)
measures style, not level or capacity
for creative problem solving

CHAPTER FIVE

What's Your Style?

"Weirdo!"

"Bean counter!"

The derogatory comments go on and on, based on how you manifest your creativity. Your creative style indicates your orientation to problem solving and the kinds of original ideas you produce.

A simple way to distinguish your probable style of creativity is to imagine that you have been given a box containing 1,000 empty tea bags. Think for a minute of all the things you could do with them. Would you stuff some tea back into them? Throw them away? Take them apart and use the string to sew the bags together into a tiny blanket with designs stapled along the edges? If you thought of ways to use them that retained their identity as tea bags, you are probably more *adaptive* in your creativity. If you transformed the tea bags into other objects, your creativity is probably more *innovative*.

The Kirton Adaption-Innovation Inventory (KAI)[1] asks you to consider how easy or difficult it is for you to consistently present yourself in certain ways. From your responses it indicates your style of creativity on a bell shaped continuum from being highly Adaptive, with a preference for *improving* existing ideas, to being highly Innovative, with a preference for *challenging* the current paradigms. Those who prefer making something better vs. those who prefer making something new. Bean counters vs. Weirdos. The KAI reflects back to Aristotle's determined and Plato's undetermined descriptions of creativity. For example, Adaptive poets prefer to write poems that rhyme in an agreed-upon structure, whether it is iambic pentameter or haiku. Innovative poets are less likely to restrict themselves to a classical writing form. They are comfortable writing in free verse. Think Longfellow vs. Walt

CHAPTER FIVE—WHAT'S YOUR STYLE? | 99

Indeed, it is the development of a style that ultimately makes an accomplished mediator.

Once the mediator has solidly established the theoretical framework, has mastered the basic principles, purpose, and methods for resolving conflict, he or she expresses these well-learned principles and techniques in the craft of mediation through a particular style.

>Donald Saposnek,
>*Style and the Family Mediator*, p. 246.

Whitman.

To understand how your style affects your thinking, imagine your brain as a very large, information-filled warehouse. If you are highly Adaptive in your creativity, this area has a long hallway with doors leading to rooms filled with filing cabinets containing the sum total of all your knowledge. If I ask you for information about, say, snowflakes, you will go down the hall in your brain to the room marked Winter. In that room you will find a filing cabinet titled Winter Precipitation. The cabinet drawers are titled Sleet, Slush, Ice, and Snow. Some are cross-referenced with Sledding and Cartoon Characters such as Frosty, Santa, The Grinch. Toward the middle of the Snow drawer is a file titled Snowflakes.

However, if you happen to be an Innovator, your brain's large knowledge warehouse does not have as many rooms as the Adaptor's. Instead, there are cubicles and some random files piled high all over the floor as well as on desks and file cabinets. To find your file on snowflakes, you might wander over in the general direction of Seasons then veer over to a pile of Winter files which includes Skis and Marshmallows, Roasting. You will rummage around for a moment till you come across the file titled Snowflakes. No problem.

If I ask you, the Adaptor, for another file, say on Palm Trees, you might respond, "Just a moment, please." You will put the Snowflake file back, close the drawer, and return to the hall, being careful to close the door to the Winter room. You will briskly walk down the hall of your brain to the door of the Biology section's Flora room, and proceed to the file cabinet marked Tropical Flora. That drawer contains the files on Palm Trees. At this point you might ask if I meant date palms or coconut palms. With that question clarified, you efficiently retrieve the correct file. That is the Adaptive mind at work.

However, if I asked you, the Innovator, for a file on Palm Trees, you will head on the diagonal directly over to your Biology section with Snowflake file still in hand, stepping over random piles of information you are intending to organize soon. After rummaging around in the Flora pile, you will pull out all the files on Palm Trees, just in case. And because you still have your Snowflakes file in hand with the Palm Trees, you can readily combine the two concepts with connections like winter escaping vacations, snow falling on palm trees, or shredded coconut. That

Snowflakes to Palm Trees

is the Innovative mind at work.

ADAPTIVE CREATIVITY

Michael Kirton's research has concluded that if you are highly Adaptive in your creativity you are considered by others to be disciplined, organized, and a careful planner. You are a stable, common sense person concerned with safety and soundness, and good at managing time and money. Although you certainly finish projects, you may be overly concerned with the *way* things get done. You tend to accept given problem definitions and are more concerned with resolving problems rather than finding them.[2] Sound familiar?

Here are more clues. You generally focus on incremental change. You prefer improving and perfecting existing systems. You are able to maintain high accuracy in long periods of detailed work.

During a KAI workshop for the staff of a wholesale tool distributor, the highest Adaptor, their inventory control manager and designated bean counter, announced that he was "boring and proud of it!" The hundred other employees gave him a standing ovation. They recognized that his Adaptive creative style made him the best man for such a detail-oriented job.

If you are an Adaptor, you are happiest working within well-established patterns and operating procedures, preferring to generate a smaller, yet for you, sufficient quantity of original ideas. Also, you prefer only those novel ideas that are most likely to be useful and relevant to the situation at hand.[3] You become an authority within a given area of expertise but might be cautious about what kinds of risks you will take. Adaptive mediators gravitate toward more structured mediations like divorce and child custody.

Recognize yourself yet? Adaptors have the hardest time convincing themselves of their own creativity. If you see yourself as an Adaptor that means it is your *style* of creativity. If you do not yet recognize your style, keep reading and see if you are more Innovative in your creativity, or if you are among the large number of those who are Middles.

INNOVATIVE CREATIVITY

High Innovators are those on the opposite end of the bell curve

... we need each other; there are too many limits on individuals working alone for them to solve most large, complex problems ... Diversity of problems requires, for their resolution, a diversity of resources, including a diversity of problem-solvers.

>Michael Kirton,
>*Adaption-Innovation: In the Context of Diversity and Change*, p. 5.

from Adaptors. If you identify yourself within this group, you are seen by others as independent, visionary, and ingenious. You prefer to think tangentially, challenging rules and procedures, existing assumptions, and established methods while advocating for novel perspectives and solutions.

If you recognize yourself as an Innovator, you "prematurely" see new problems and can take control in unstructured, chaotic situations. You are knowledgeable in a wide range of areas, extremely flexible with change, are unconstrained by limited resources, and prefer flexible work habits. In the extreme, you are seen by those more Adaptive in their creativity as a risk-taker irreverent of the consensus views of settled groups, and unwilling to conform to group norms. An Innovator mediator friend expresses frustration at always seeming to be in trouble with both her partner and children.

As an Innovator you may be undisciplined in your work habits and have a low tolerance for detailed, routine work. You create change for the sake of change and seem to have little concern for the practicality or soundness of a new idea. You may prefer to stay in "process" with little regard for eventual outcome.[4] Does this describe anyone you know?

My initial introduction to the KAI was in Buffalo. When I took the KAI I could see where my scores were heading so I did the only reasonable thing to do—I cheated. I knew that those I met during my first week of grad school were probably the only friends I would have for the duration of my time there and I was already considered different just for being from "Orygone."

The possible range of scores is 30-160. I fudged enough on the responses to bring my score down to 135, the highest score my advisor had ever seen. A year later, my cover as a high Innovator already blown, I retook the KAI and scored closer to 155. I say closer because really high Innovators don't care about specific numbers anyway.

When shown the KAI instructions, high Innovators may even challenge *them*, declaring that the KAI styles bell curve should bend back around on itself. Innovators are not at just one extreme. They can adapt to the point that they alternate between the two extremes. I know high Innovators who resent always being the ones who have to adapt to the Adaptors. When asked to complete the survey, one high Innovator burst into tears at what

> ... both adaptors and innovators are creative in different preferred ways and can operate in any field of activity ... The bias against adaptive creativity abounds in the creativity literature. Mostly ... it is denied altogether; sometimes it is admitted but treated as inferior to what is deemed (correctly or otherwise) as innovative creativity ...
>
> Michael Kirton,
> *Adaption-Innovation: In the Context of Diversity and Change*, p. 139.

she considered the absurdity of being asked how easy *or* difficult something was. "They should make up their freakin' minds!" No need for her to continue. By challenging the basic premise of the survey, she had already demonstrated her highly Innovative creative style.

During my initial KAI training, led by Michael Kirton himself, I was flatly told that high Innovators were not capable of being good mediators. Kirton assumed that serious communication difficulties automatically occur between people with greater than 20-point differences in their scores. Of course I couldn't resist the challenge. For the duration of the four-day workshop, to the amusement of my fellow grad students, I informally mediated between Kirton and the others as they challenged his theory and definitions. "So what I'm hearing you say is ..."

MIDDLES

If you recognize parts of yourself in *both* the Adaptor and Innovator descriptions, you probably manifest, in moderation, characteristics at each end of the bell curve, without the extreme behavior of either. You are versatile, flexible in your thinking and in relationships with others. Middles have a moderate tolerance for ambiguity. You can either work within given structures or create a new one, according to the situational need. Adaptors might see you as fairly radical while Innovators might see you as more staid.[5]

As a Middle you work well with a wide range of people and ideas. You can generate many different perspectives and tend to have a greater awareness of different qualities of a problem. You are capable of providing either needed details or generate novel ideas, depending on what the situation demands. And you are likely to have productive results from your efforts. You are able to use a broad range of criteria for consensus decision making and are capable of offering specific action steps toward completion of a task.

On the other hand, when generating ideas in a group, you may become self-conscious about others' reactions. You may be less willing to contribute extreme ideas unless encouraged to do so. Middles can get caught up in observing the dynamics of the two extreme styles and may, in fact, become invisible. You may be too focused on the middle ground, unwilling to consider either

... mediators need to find an individual style that is congruent with their personal qualities and plays to their strengths, rather than imitating the styles of others.... a variety of styles, techniques, and methods of mediation have proven to be effective, in large part because so much depends on hard-to-define, and therefore hard-to-prescribe, personal elements.

>Daniel Bowling & David Hoffman,
>*Bringing Peace into the Room*, pp. 2-3.

the usefulness or novelty found at either end of the Adaptive/Innovative bell curve.

Another way to establish your probable style is by joining in this highly improbable scenario that I present during Creative Styles workshops. Pretend for a moment that you are the member of an intact work group who just completed a huge project on time and under budget. The company owner wants to reward your group by allowing you to spend the saved $5000 on yourselves, as a group, any way you want. What ideas would you propose? In one particularly memorable workshop, the highest Innovator group planned a weekend trip to Vegas for the bunch of them, complete with gambling money and massages. Meanwhile, the highest Adaptor group voted to buy Post-it notes and other supplies for their office!

Coping skills are necessary when there is a gap between your preferred style and the situational requirements on your actual behavior.[6] Although your style does not change, your behavior can. However, it takes more energy to function outside your style and can be more tiring to concentrate on how to act. As a high Innovator, I have developed all sorts of strategies for being effective with those to my left on the bell curve. When teaching I now routinely tidy my desk area, after a high Adapter student once rushed up during a break to straighten my mess, saying it was so distracting that she could not concentrate on the discussion. Also, like other Innovators, I tend to make use of lots of metaphors to make a point, which can lose more literalist Adaptors. I encourage students to interrupt me to ask for clarification when I just don't make sense to them. And, I really do try to finish my sentences ... Things like that.

People with a preference for ...

... Extraversion (E) direct their energy *outward* in action.

... Introversion (I) direct their energy *inward* in reflection.

... Sensing (S) pay attention to *specifics* presented by their five senses.

... Intuition (N) pay attention to *meanings* and *patterns* presented by memory and association.

... Thinking (T) make decisions through logical analysis, objective and impersonal criteria. They seek rational order through *logic*.

... Feeling (F) make decisions through subjective criteria that weigh values and motives. They seek rational order through *harmony*.

... Judging (J) like deciding, planning, organizing and scheduling. They *want closure*, even when information is incomplete.

... Perceiving (P) prefer inquiring, absorbing, and adapting. They *resist closure*, always seeming to want more information.

>Isabel Briggs Myers, Mary McCaulley, Naomi Quenk, & Allen Hammer, *Manual: A Guide to the Development and Use of the Myers-Briggs Type Indicator*, pp. 336-337.

CHAPTER SIX

What's Your Type?

"All this talk of emotions makes me want to puke!"

A mediator blurted this during a MBTI for Mediators Workshop I once presented. I will get to what caused that outburst in a moment. First, some background information.

Your uniqueness as a human being is determined by a combination of things; your gender, ethnicity, personality, age, eye color, creative level and style, even your shoe size, plus a host of other physical, mental and psychological characteristics. The combination of traits revealed by the Myers Briggs Type Indicator (MBTI) contributes to that list. It is yet another way to look at your attributes as a creative person. The MBTI explains your creativity in terms of how you take in information and how you make decisions based on that information.

I was introduced to the MBTI, the granddaddy of all personality type instruments, during graduate school as a method for viewing the creative person. Soon after that I became qualified to administer and interpret it. Here is what I was taught.

The MBTI was designed to make Carl Jung's theory of psychological types understandable and useful in people's lives. MBTI theory holds that "much seemingly random behavior is actually quite orderly and consistent; due to basic differences in the way people prefer to use their perception and judgment."[1]

Like left or right handedness, we all tend to use and more fully develop the skills and processes we are most comfortable with. Although you are able to write with your less-dominant hand, the result is less controlled, looks a little ragged, and takes more effort to make legible.

As with creative styles, you might recognize your type just from reading the following descriptors from the *MBTI Manual*.[2] Your response to questions in the *Workbook* will also give you a

... almost everything people do with their minds is an act of perception or an act of judgment. Succeeding at anything takes both perception and judgment and in that order. Before people can rightly decide how to handle a situation they must find out what the problem is and what the alternatives are. Finding out is an exercise of perception, and deciding is an exercise of judgment.

Isabel Briggs Myers, *Gifts Differing*, p. 199.

quick snapshot of your probable type. This chapter provides just enough of an overview of the MBTI to allow a discussion of its application to mediation. If you decide you want to complete the entire MBTI, a list of qualified practitioners is available through www.DiscoverYourPersonality.com. Books for further reading are also listed in the Chapter Notes at the end of *Picasso*.

Now, imagine you are attending one of my MBTI workshops. You have completed the Myers-Briggs Type Indicator. There has been a brief explanation of the theory behind it, very much like what you just read. I show a list of attributes on the screen. The lights dim ...

EXTRAVERSION / INTROVERSION

Extraverts (E) direct their energy outward in action. They seek stimulation, ideas, and values in their *outer* environment. Introverts (I), on the other hand, direct their energy *inward* in reflection. They seek stimulation, ideas and values in their *inner* mental environment. Extraverts like variety and action, having others around, and phone conversations. Often they seem impetuous, acting quickly without thinking. They are sometimes impatient with long slow jobs. Extraverts need to *talk* in order to *think*, so they think out loud. Their words need to leave their mouths and enter their brains through their ears. Extraverts comprise approximately 75% of the US population, so not only do Extraverts talk too much, but as some Introverts will tell you, there are too *many* of them.

Conversely, Introverts need to *think* in order to *talk*. They can form whole paragraphs in their minds, then have to decide *which* paragraph to speak. Introverts report impatience with Extraverts' constant verbal observations, running commentaries, and general chatter.

Introverts are more comfortable with silence and tend to wait to speak until they have something they consider relevant to say. Introverts like quiet for concentration, prefer communications to be in writing, and can work contentedly alone on a single project for quite a long time. No interruptions or phone calls please. They can ponder an action for a long time, sometimes without acting on it at all.

At my MBTI workshops, after showing the overhead descriptions of each scale, I ask everyone to participate in a tried-and-

Conflicting Definitions of Conflict

Thinkers: Any discussion, conversation, or debate when win/lose is the only perceivable possible outcome.

Feelers: Conflict exists when we have four sets of opinions/feelings, ideas/experiences, and we're trying to reach consensus.

>   Otto Kroeger & Janet Thuesen,
>   *Type Talk*, p. 106.

true exercise that allows them to validate their type in their own experience. Those who are willing divide into groups of Introverts and Extraverts. The two groups are asked to generate three questions to ask the other group. (What questions come to your mind?) Two distinct things happen. One is that the Introverted bunch is silent as they individually consider the questions. The other is that the Extraverted group is immediately chaotic as everyone talks at once. The other invariable response is that when time is up, neither group has generated a list of questions! The Introverts are still thinking about them while the Extraverts had lots of questions but did not get around to writing theirs down. After their chuckles of recognition, I provide a few more minutes for each group to complete their task.

The resulting workshop questions that cause the greatest insights are variations on "Why do you *talk* so much?" (from the Introverts) and "What are you *thinking*?" (from the Extraverts.) The most contentious question came from an Extraverted group who probed, "Aren't you Introverts really just repressed Extraverts?" Pandemonium ensued! A few disgusted Introverts threatened to walk out.

SENSING / INTUITION

At this point in a workshop I always note that the letter "N" is used as an abbreviated term for "intuitive" because the "I" already has been taken by the word "introvert." Now back to the slides.

The Sensing/Intuition scale describes two ways of perceiving the world; all the ways of taking in information and becoming aware of your surroundings. Sensing (S) people prefer to pay attention to specifics presented by their five senses. They are most aware of the facts and details of their present experience. Intuitives (N), on the other hand, pay attention to meanings and patterns presented by their memory and association. They are more aware of possibilities, imaginings, and insights. The facts need not always apply.

Sensors are aware of the uniqueness of each event and accept current reality as it is. They are careful about the facts of a situation. They like established ways of doing things and tend to focus on what works now. Sensors can work steadily at a task with a realistic idea of how long it will take. They prefer to reach a conclusion by working through a situation step by step and may

Psychological Diversity

There are ... differences in how people organize and process information as an expression of their cognitive styles and personality traits ... There might be two individuals who possess the same primary forms of diversity, yet who are completely opposite with regard to their personalities ...

Gerard Puccio, Mary Murdock, & Marie Mance,
Creative Leadership: Skills That Drive Change,
pp. 205-206.

oversimplify a task. They are considered practical, down-to-earth, sensible, realistic folks. They often are the people who run our businesses, banks, and government agencies. While Sensing people make up about 75% of the U.S. population, very few self-select to become mediators.

In contrast, the 25% of the population who have a preference for Intuition dislike redundant activities or taking time for precision, even while they may over-complexify a task. They follow their inspirations and hunches, causing them to get their facts a bit wrong, which does not seem to greatly trouble them. Because they like new challenges and possibilities they sometimes challenge the status quo. They work in bursts of energy powered by enthusiasm, with slack periods in between. Words that describe Intuitives include imaginative, speculative, head-in-clouds, and ingenuity. They choose fiction over fact, fantasy over utility. These people become the artists, actors, entrepreneurs, philosophers, poets, adventurers, and, overwhelmingly, mediators.

A great workshop exercise for this scale has people in their groups write words and phrases that describe "apple." Lists from Sensors begin with sensing words; things they can see, feel, taste, hear or smell, like "crunchy, tart, sweet, red, green." Then they branch out into words like "Macintosh, Granny Smith, pie, turnover, Delicious, tree, and orchard." After a while someone may branch out to say "computer."

Meanwhile, the Intuitives' list often begins with "computer," then moves to chip, potato, micro, poker, and beyond. Sometimes the list begins with William Tell and moves from there to "arrow, Robin Hood, neighborhood, block party, garage sale, overture, and Middle Ages." After they have exhausted the more obscure connections, they will drop back to sensing words like "crunchy, pie and delicious." Were the words you thought of more Sensing or Intuitive?

Of the fifty participants at a particularly memorable MBTI for Mediators Workshop, we discovered that only two were in the Sensing group. Their apple list was pretty thin. I divided the other forty eight Intuitives into eight small groups of six, resulting in multiple random lists of words to describe "apple." They had a ball while the two token Sensors sat quietly by wondering how the Intuitives got from Robin Hood to garage sale.

NF Temperament: Idealist

Idealists tend to be gifted at unifying diverse people and helping individuals realize their potential. They build bridges between people through empathy and clarification of deeper issues. They use these same skills to help people work through difficulties. Thus they can make excellent mediators, helping people and companies solve conflicts through mutual cooperation.

> Isabel Briggs Myers, Mary McCaulley, Naomi Quenk, & Allen Hammer,
> *Manual: A Guide to the Development and Use of the Myers-Briggs Type Indicator*, p. 332.

THINKING / FEELING

Back at my generic MBTI workshop, I move on to slides about the next scale, Thinking (T) and Feeling (F). These are two essential ways of making rational judgments, and where the English translation of Carl Jung's 1923 work in German causes problems. I always mention as an aside that "Thinking" does not mean "unemotional" and "Feeling" does not mean "emotional." Conclusions reached by an emotional reaction are not rational. Because of the dated translation, it is necessary to suspend normal English definitions when using these words in terms of the MBTI. Think of the current appropriation of everyday words for computer applications; your computer "mouse" moving the curser around your "desktop."

Back to the PowerPoint. People with a preference for Thinking make decisions through the use of logical analysis, objective and impersonal criteria. They seek rational order through *logic*. With their ability to put things in logical order, Thinkers have a talent for analyzing a problem or situation. They can anticipate or predict the logical outcomes of the choices they make. Those with a preference for Thinking tend to be firm and tough-minded; more able to reprimand or fire people when necessary. They respond more to people's ideas than to their feelings and may hurt someone's feelings without even knowing it. When making decisions, Thinking types take existing laws and standards, justice, principles, and policies into consideration. Do those descriptors sound familiar?

Feelers, on the other hand, use personal values and priorities to make decisions; subjective criteria that weigh human values and motives. They seek rational order through *harmony*. They are good at seeing the effects choices have on people. They enjoy pleasing people, and tend to be sympathetic. They also need occasional praise. They take an interest in the person behind the job and respond to people's values as much as to their thoughts. They tend to be devoted, persuasive, and humane. They consider social values and extenuating circumstances as part of their decision making process. Anybody you know?

There is a gender split between the numbers of Thinkers and Feelers in the U.S. population. Females make up approximately 40% of Thinkers but 60% of Feelers, with males, of course, being the opposite. This fact accounts for those who go against

SJ Temperament: Guardian

Guardians need to know they are doing the responsible thing. They value stability, security, and a sense of community. They trust hierarchy and authority and may be surprised when others go against these. Guardians prefer cooperative actions with a focus on standards and norms. Their orientation is to their past experiences, and they like things sequenced and structured.

> Isabel Briggs Myers, Mary McCaulley, Naomi Quenk, & Allen Hammer,
> *Manual: A Guide to the Development and Use of the Myers-Briggs Type Indicator*, p. 332.

stereotypes, like the "good guy" sensitive male and the "hard-as-nails" tough female.

The usual exercise for this scale is to divide people into groups and ask them to list how they like to show appreciation to others and how they like appreciation shown to them. Again, there are a couple of standard responses. One is that those with a Feeling preference like to be hugged, while Thinkers cringe at the thought. The other universal response has to do with praise for workplace accomplishments. Thinkers consider praise for "just doing their job" insincere. They are incredulous when they hear Feelers report that they want appreciation shown to them for just being who they are. They ask if Feelers really expect to be appreciated for just showing up at their jobs, without even having done any work. The Feelers' defensive response: "Actually, yes, we do."

In the MBTI for Mediators Workshop, again there were only two lonely Thinkers among the 48 Feeling types. It was when the conversation moved to the importance of allowing emotions during mediations that one of the Thinking participants blurted, "All this talk of emotions makes me want to puke!" Well now, that sure opened up a whole conversation about mediator impartiality, a topic we will get to in the next chapter.

Meanwhile, back to the generic Myers-Briggs workshop ...

JUDGMENT / PERCEPTION

Judging (J) and Perceiving (P) are two attitudes for dealing with your outer environment. Here again the translation from German causes problems. "Perception," as used here, includes all the ways you become aware of things, people, happenings or ideas, while "judgment" includes all the ways you come to conclusions about what you perceived. Judging does not mean "judgmental" and "Perceiving" does not mean "perceptive" as an attribute of maturity or intelligence. Both types are found in equal numbers within the United States population.

People with a preference for Judging like the physical act of deciding, planning, organizing and scheduling. They want closure, even when information is incomplete. Judgers like to plan ahead, be in charge of their lives. They work best when they can plan their work and follow their plan. Because they like to get things settled and finished, they may decide things too quickly and tend to end

> Too many individuals come away from their exposure to the MBTI thinking that their results are better or worse than others, or that type necessarily causes behavior ...
>
> It's an abuse of type theory to use it to excuse unacceptable behavior,... to explain poor performance,... to blame others,... to project onto others' motivations, and to predict individual competencies.
>
> Roger Pearman & Sarah Albritton,
I'm Not Crazy, I'm Just Not You, p. 162.

further consideration of the subject once they reach a judgment. Judging types want only the essentials needed to begin their work and may dislike interrupting the project they are working on for a more urgent one. Judgers use lists as tools for action.

In contrast, Perceivers prefer to stay in the act of inquiring, absorbing, and adapting. They adapt well to changing situations and do not mind leaving things open for the last minute. Those with a preference for Perceiving resist closure, always seeming to want more information. They have squishy mental boundaries about time. They start more projects than can be reasonably completed within a given timeframe. They tend to postpone unpleasant jobs, and have difficulty finishing them. Yet they get a lot accomplished at the last minute under pressure of a deadline. They are content when things are pending, emergent, and flexible. Perceivers use lists as reminders of all the things they have to do someday.

People in workshops validate their Judging/Perceiving preference by lining up on a continuum according to their response to a question I ask in two very different ways. The first way is "To what extent can you do what you *want* to do before you finish what you *have* to do?" Depending on the strength of their preference, Judgers may reply, "Never, I always finish my work before I play." Meanwhile, Perceivers do not even understand the question. So I reframe it into, "To what extent do you have to get all your work done before you can play?" Perceivers are all over that question. Those with a strong preference for Perceiving report that they can stop for a break at any time, for any reason. And that it is all play or they avoid getting involved in the first place.

Secondary workshop questions include how often each group cleans their desks or their cars, and how far ahead of leaving do they need to pack for a trip. The continuum goes from those Judgers who pack weeks in advance to those Perceivers who do not pack at all, but buy new clothes when they arrive at their destination!

By the end of the MBTI for Mediators Workshop with only the two Sensors, I knew I was on to something important. The composite MBTI scores were fully documented on the white board at the back of the room and I was already planning the article I wanted to write on this new Blinding Flash of the Obvious. However, as I was answering the last question asked by the last participant, the dutiful Judging staff person efficiently and

MBTI Applications to Mediation

Your type affects:

1. The kinds of mediation you gravitate toward, the methods and techniques you prefer, and your preference for different approaches: evaluative, facilitative, transformative, or hybrid.

2. Your interaction with each of the parties based on the dynamic between your type and their types.

3. Your ability to facilitate communication between the disputing parties based on their type differences.

completely erased the entire MBTI chart from the white board! Somehow I managed to give her a weak thanks for her efficient tidiness before I wandered off, inconsolable over my lost data.

So there you have it. Now that you have attended my virtual workshop and read research on the subject, what do you predict is your type?

I have collected type scores from 92 Oregon mediators who reported their scores from other MBTI workshops. (See the *Workbook* for more details.) Like those at the MBTI for Mediators Workshop, an overwhelming 85% of the mediators had preference for Intuition, compared to 27% of the general population. Over 50% of these mediators had a preference for Intuition *and* Feeling, compared to 16% of the general population. Further, 25% of the responding mediators reported a preference for a single type, ENFP (Extraverted, iNtuitive, Feeling, Perceiving). As an ENFP myself, I am not at all surprised.

TYPE, POSITIVITY AND CREATIVE STYLES

An Ego-Resiliency Scale[3] looks at personalities from a different angle. It uses responses to targeted questions as a measure and prediction of resilient personality styles. The scale has shown that people with more resilient personalities rebound from adversity only to the extent that they generally experienced higher than average positivity. So the more positivity you generate in your life, the more resilient you are. I suspect that mediators score high on the resiliency scale. As *Positivity* author Fredrickson explains[4]

> This pattern of data tells us people with resilient personality styles are indeed emotionally responsive. They are not disconnected, head-in-sand, unflappable robots. They are moved just like the rest of us. But when circumstances suddenly change for the better, they are quick to move on. They let go. Positivity makes them nimble. More than others, people with resilient personality styles put the "undo effect" of positivity to work. They bounce back—even at a core physiological level—because their inner wellspring of positive emotions bubbles over. Positivity serves as their secret "reset" button.

According to Fredrickson, people with more positivity become "more optimistic, more resilient, more open, more accepting and more driven by purpose."[5] That sounds like self-actualizing, creative mediators.

... it appears that the one weakness in mediation, in reference to the types of personalities it attracts as mediators, is the lack of preference for perceiving concrete data. According to the theory, this includes attention to detail. This ... could mean overlooked facts and/or problems, and ultimately might result in weak agreements. The good news is that those who prefer the opposite, or more abstract kind of perception, also like to think of possibilities. This makes them strong on options and we all know how important that is to a successful mediation.

> Lyn Wade,
> *Mediation and Personality Type*, pp. 4-5.

As you might suspect, there are also correlations between personality types (MBTI) and creative styles (KAI). Recall that the KAI measures your orientation to creativity and problem solving; the kinds of information you pay attention to, how you collect and analyze that data, and how you choose to use the information. Think back to where you sense you placed yourself on the KAI continuum of creative styles—Adaptive, Middle, Innovative.

Studies have found correlations between creative styles and type, especially between the MBTI Sensing-Intuitive and Judging-Perceiving scales.[6] For all you Sensing folks, here are the stats: A 70% correlation was found between KAI and the Sensing-Intuitive scales, and 20% correlation was found between the KAI and the Judging-Perceiving scales. This means that Adaptors generally prefer Sensing (S) and Judging (J) while Innovators generally prefer Intuition (N) and Perception (P). It follows then, that the more Adaptive you are, the more likely you are to have a Sensing/Judging type preference. The stronger your Innovator score, the more likely you are to have an Intuitive/Perceiving type preference. How does that match your experience?

It seems reasonable to assume that your personality type affects the kinds of mediation you gravitate toward, the methods and techniques you prefer, and your preference for different mediation approaches: evaluative, facilitative, transformative, or hybrid. Your interaction with each of the parties is also affected by the dynamic between your type and their types.

Innovative mediators who share preferences for both Intuition and Perceiving are no doubt more comfortable with the expansive aspects of the creative process. (More on creative processes in Chapter Ten: In Defense of Problem Solving.) That matches the responses to exercises in my MBTI workshops. Intuitives sure sound Innovative in their variety of apple descriptors. Sensors are much more Adaptive in their apple descriptions. You Adaptive mediators, with your preferences for both Sensing and Judging, probably excel more at the decision making aspect of the creative process. Note: both scales are needed for creative thinking and both are needed in mediation. Adaptive mediators just need to relax more with the unstructured "sticky middle part"[7] while Innovators need to be sure to cover all the structured elements of mediation: opening statements and the details of agreement writing.

Questions to Ask Each Preference

Sensing (S)
- What insights and hunches do you have?
- What other directions can be explored?
- What does this situation remind you of?

Intuition (N)
- What are the facts?
- What exactly is the situation now?
- What already exists and works?

Thinking (T)
- How will the outcome affect you?
- What is your personal reaction to each alternative?
- How will others respond to the options?

Feeling (F)
- What are the pros and cons of each situation?
- What objective criteria needs to be satisfied?
- What is the most reasonable course of action?

> Adapted from Sandra Hirsh & Jean Kummerow,
> *Introduction to Type in Organizations*, p. 31.

JUGGLING TYPE THEORY

Having learned about type, conflict, and creativity theories, all within a tight time-frame, it is natural for me to think of type's applications to mediation. I understand the type-related reasons why I prefer some kinds of mediations over others, and how to maintain at least my perceived impartiality if a party rubs me the wrong way. Knowledge of type helps me get a handle on the parties' interests, and how to better respond to them.

Self-knowledge of your own type can also help you in these same three distinct areas. If you are a mediator with a preference for Sensing, you probably excel at the kinds of disputes that require attention to financial and scheduling details, like divorce and child custody cases. Those of you with a preference for Intuition gravitate to other kinds of mediation. If you have a preference for Thinking decision making you help bring clarity to issues of justice. If you have a Feeling decision making preference you are more apt to focus on extenuating circumstances. Judging mediators tend to be more outcome-oriented, keeping things on track within a tight time-frame. Perceivers tend to be more process oriented, delving into the details of the disputed situation, finding areas of common agreement. Can you see both the strengths and challenges your creative style and personality type brings to your mediation practice?

Juggling is a handy metaphor for type applications to mediation. Apples, for example, might represent your own type and your impartiality. While you are tossing your apples in the air, add a degree of difficulty by throwing in a watermelon, representing your response to the parties' personality types. The challenge is to juggle both of those elements, especially as you increase your ability to uncover conflicts caused by *their* type differences. Now let's add a bunch of grapes to your apples and watermelon juggling act. They represent your increased ability to facilitate communication between the parties.

The challenge for you as a creative mediator is to concurrently keep everything in the air; the apples of your perceived impartiality, the watermelon of your own MBTI type and its relationship to the parties, and the grapes of the parties' relationship to each other. Awareness of type enables you to reframe a party's evident emotion or frustration into type theory, normalizing the behavior as "just hard wiring" rather than a personal attack. Highlighting

Juggling Type Theory

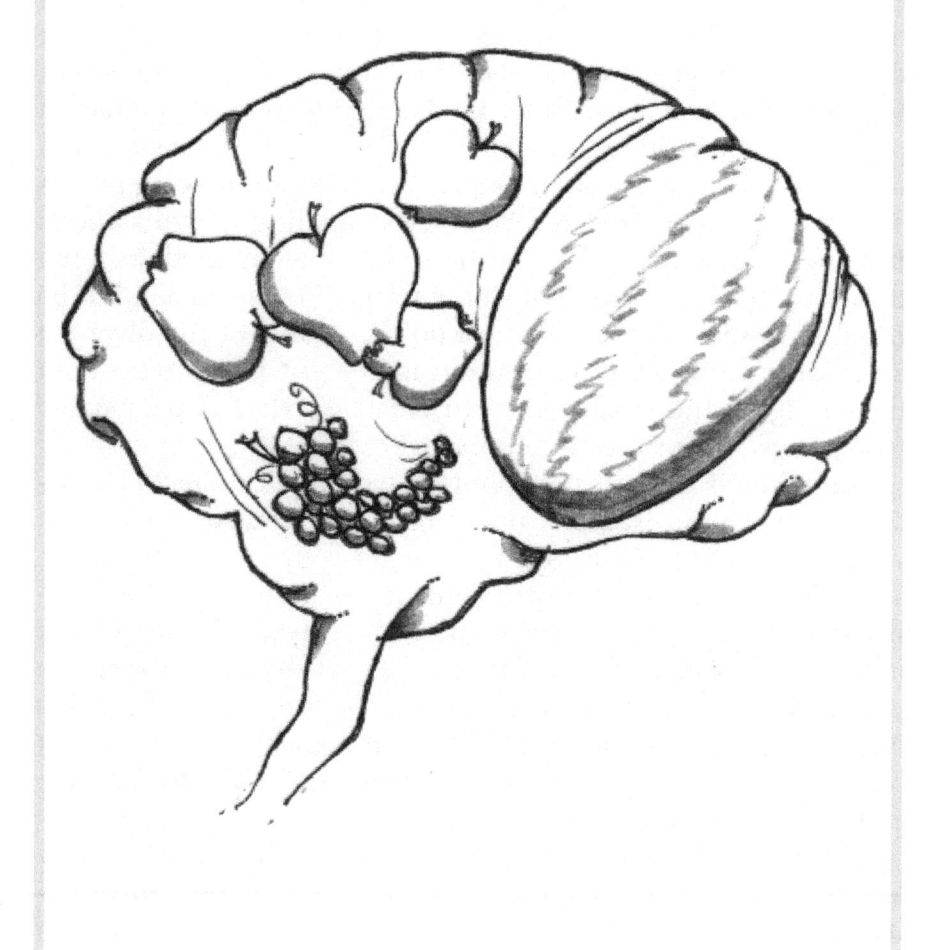

the conflict through the type lens can assist the parties in considering a wider variety of options for developing solutions and new avenues for reconciliation.

Regardless of what MBTI type you consider yourself, your task is still to keep everything in the air. You simultaneously flex to match both parties' types, maintain the integrity of the process, and provide a safe place where they can risk exploring creative solutions to entrenched problems ... all at once.

Myers-Briggs personality type information might prompt you to juggle with a co-mediator with opposite strengths. If you are Extraverted, an Introverted co-mediator could balance you by taking notes and drafting agreement language while you question the parties. Introverted mediators excel at thinking over situations, and then making the exact thoughtful overarching comments that help parties find commonality. If you fit that description you might benefit by co-mediating with Extraverted mediators who are verbally quick on their feet.

Again, if you are new to the MBTI, take your time. You will not develop your type-juggling skills overnight. Some people spend their entire lives studying type theory. Give yourself time to absorb the information gleaned from your own type before attempting to integrate it in your mediation practice.

You will probably begin by having some small glimpses of insight into type's value during mediations. This became very apparent to me as I attended an all-day workshop on the MBTI for mediators. In the morning we explored our own type and, in the afternoon, attempted to apply it to mediation. Those unfamiliar with type theory were lost. The afternoon found them still back processing their *own* types, nowhere near having assimilated the information enough to begin juggling.

Up to now *Picasso* has been about you as a self-actualizing, positive, creative person. Hopefully, you have undone some limiting beliefs and accept that you are indeed creative, and you have a sense of your creative style and type. Armed with new information about yourself, the question now is, what are you going to do with it? In what ways might you incorporate it into your mediation practice? To answer these questions, *Picasso* continues to shift from you as a creative individual to you as a creative mediator.

CHAPTER SIX—WHAT'S YOUR TYPE? | 131

> Metaphorical imagination is a crucial skill in creating rapport and in communicating the nature of unshared experience. This skill consists ... of the ability to bend your world view and adjust the way you categorize your experience. Problems of mutual understanding are not exotic; they arise in all extended conversations where understanding is important.
>
> > George Lakoff & Mark Johnson,
> > *Metaphors We Live By*, p. 231.

CHAPTER SEVEN

Values, Metaphors, and Impartiality

"The guy was really a jerk!"

As a newbie back in 1985, during a meeting of the newly formed Mediation Guild I was shocked to hear a mediator say such a thing about one of the parties. As a freshly minted, very naïve mediator, I placed all mediators on a very high pedestal. I assumed that their impartiality was constant, complete, and beyond reproach. Yet during the debriefing someone I greatly admired from afar was making a derogatory comment about a mediation client! Others chimed in their various opinions and judgments. I couldn't believe my ears. How unseemly! It was shocking, I say, shocking!

Only later did I realize it was *my* pedestal they were falling from, and they had nowhere to go but down. My severe judgment was quite unfair to the mere mortals in the room. It took me awhile to realize the extent to which mediation is the art of *perceived* impartiality. Mediators still operate within their own value systems. As my mediator friend Jon Townsend often says, "The only neutral beings are asexual penguins."

As we begin the focus on you as a creative mediator, there is the need to examine the extent to which all the aspects of your creativity operate within the boundaries of your cultural and personal values. Which, in turn, affect your impartiality.

Take a look at the Values Inventory in the *Workbook*. At first glance the values probably seem equally important. But as you complete the Inventory, you will be able to thoughtfully examine your internal reaction to each value presented. It is a fairly accurate way to assess some of your most and least important values.

One way to approach the concept of values is to spend some time at the intersection of neuroscience and metaphor. What we call "values" are the result of an accumulation of unconscious

Metaphors on the Mind

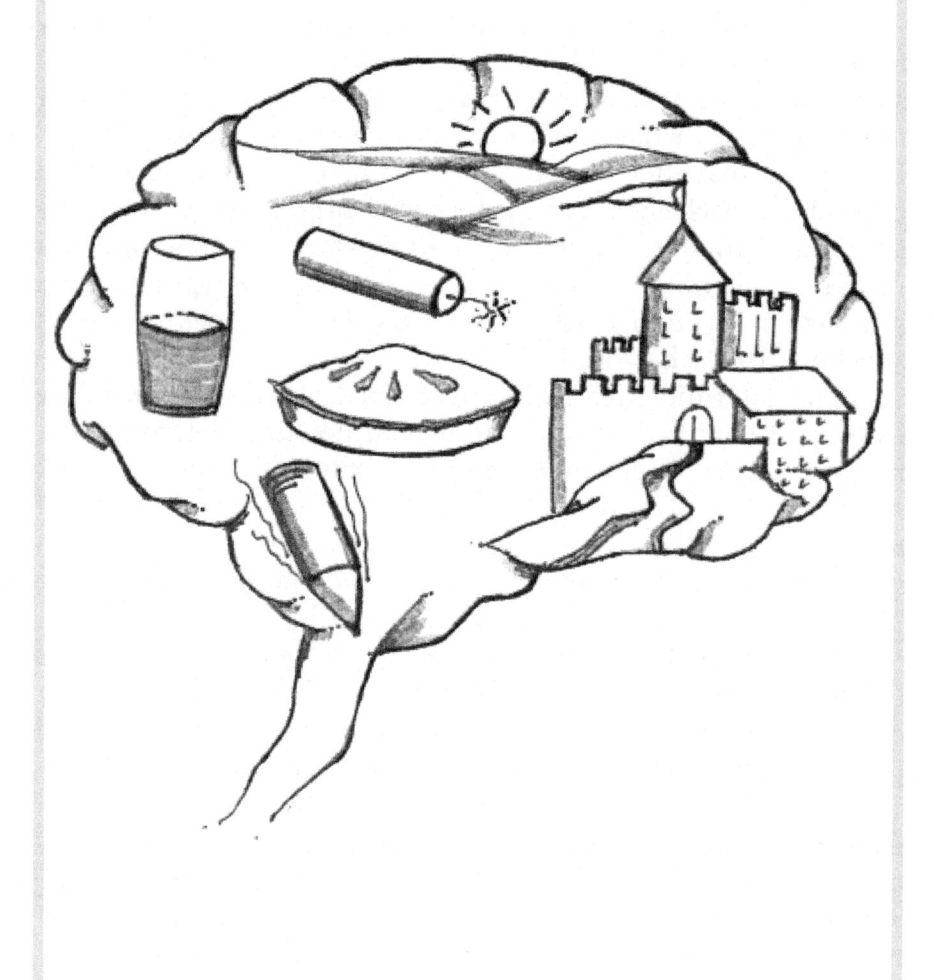

primary metaphors from which you "naturally" operate. These hardwired metaphors are embedded deep in the synapses of your brain. At least 95% of all your thought is below consciousness, inaccessible to conscious control, yet shaping all your conscious thought. As an infant you did not know the difference between subjective experiences and your judgments concerning them so your brain automatically and unconsciously acquired a vast number of concrete (physical, solid) metaphors that allowed you to understand abstract concepts. For example, the early *subjective* experience of love and affection is typically correlated with the *sensory* experience of warmth. Even after you grew up to cognitively know the difference, the association persists as a "warm smile." These experiences developed into widespread conceptual metaphors because they are *physically* realized in your brain; they are hardwired.[1]

English is awash with metaphors, both in thought and language. They allow you to experience one kind of thing in terms of another, from apples and oranges to nuts and bolts. You cut to the chase, fish or cut bait, bite the bullet, describe water to a fish. English is so filled with metaphors that you hardly notice the shared meanings they provide. Think back to the juggling metaphor in the previous chapter. You just go with the flow, don't rock the boat, keep your head above water, and sink or swim come hell or high water. You tackle sticky problems, make an end run, or pinch hit to left field, to mix a few.

The usefulness of metaphors depends on their shared meaning. Your Reticular Activating System tunes in to metaphorical blips on its radar, allowing it to make appropriate connections. While an American worries about sticking out like a sore thumb, a self-conscious Chinese feels like a crane among chickens.

The very concept of "understanding" is dependent on metaphors. They allow you to use the physical logic of grasping or holding on in order to think about the abstract concept of "understanding." You conceptualize the understanding of an idea, a subject experience, in terms of grasping an object, a concrete physical experience. If you understand the idea you get a handle on it. If you do not understand, you can't get a grip on it, or it's out of reach.[2]

Knowing this, the first exercise in my mediation course is for small groups to draw out the mediation process as a map.

> We acquire a large system of primary metaphors automatically and unconsciously from our earliest years. Because of the way neural connections are formed in early life we all naturally use hundreds of primary metaphors in order to think.
>
> George Lakoff & Mark Johnson,
> *Philosophy in the Flesh*, p. 47.

They combine the abstract concept of "mediation process" with the concrete concept of "map." Over the years there have been a remarkable variety of responses, from pirates' hidden treasure maps to garbage truck routes. Yet when asked for their insights based on the exercise, they get it. They uniformly report their new realization that they need to follow the process, and that they cannot use "short cuts."

The idea of a "catchment" provides another metaphorical explanation of how metaphors affect your values and impartiality. While actual physical water catchments are very wide collection basin areas that water flows into, metaphorical catchments are mental funneling systems that constrict a wide variety of inputs to the same output.[3] Some words are so common that people assume the words have a shared meaning. Tall buildings are categorized as "skyscrapers," while some domesticated animals are categorized as "dogs" others are "cats." Some concepts have very broad catchment areas and readily become unconscious mental traps. In mediation, catchment terms such as "loud," "fair," "choice," "music," and "truth," are often fighting words.

We all mentally categorize how we think of things. Most categories are matters of degree, such as "tall people." There are also graded concepts within degrees, like "normal," and "not quite normal." Because of their assumed shared meaning, these are the kinds of catchment words that cause conflict. For example, how many is many? How many is several? How low is low?

Assumptions about what is "low" caused a fascinating dispute between two medical receptionists, both responsible for maintaining a steady supply of blank files available for new patient intake. These files were kept on the counter under a cabinet. During the mediation I realized that they seemed to have different definitions of "low." When I asked the receptionists what "low" meant to them, one said that the stack of files was "low" when she could not cram one more file under the cabinet. For the other, "low" meant they were down to the last ten files on the stack.

Based on these differing definitions they had built up all sorts of other negative assumptions about the other, resulting in terms like "slacker" and "bean counter." Once they became aware of their differing perceptions of "low," they were able to untangle other definitions and assumptions about each other's attitudes

> One does not ... merely think about an idea ... one wrestles with it, grapples with it, coaxes it, toys with it, plays with it, beats it in the ground, hammers on it, hits it on the head, buys it, swallows it, digests it, absorbs it.
>
> Stephen Axley,
> *Managerial and Organizational Communication in Terms of the Conduit Metaphor*, p. 429.

and intentions, resulting in their eventual reconciliation.

Surprisingly, we believe hardwired metaphors before we believe official definitions. Not only that, but sometimes the official institutionalized definitions themselves are common misconceptions that become their *own* catchment traps. For example, the dictionary defines "communication" as "... a process by which information is exchanged between individuals ..."[4] The inclusion of the word "exchanged" in the definition mistakenly assumes that the listener is essential to the understanding of the speaker, implying that there is an *exchange* of ideas and information. Intellectually, that makes sense, but metaphorically, it just doesn't fly.

Unconscious, hard-wired metaphors for "communication" focus only on the speaker, minimizing the listener. Common one-way lines include:

- You heard what I said!
- How many times do I have to tell you?
- If I've told you once, I've told you a thousand times ...
- I *told* you what was wrong. Weren't you listening?

THE CONDUIT METAPHOR

The conduit metaphor is the culprit. It's the most pervasive communication metaphor in the English language.[5] Like the meat grinder and other metaphors for abstract concepts, the conduit metaphor expresses "communication" in concrete terms, as if it were a pipeline; a container with an interior and exterior. In reality, it puts communication on a one-way street (to mix yet another one). While official definitions of "communication" emphasize the responsibility of the listener, the conduit metaphor, instead, implicitly emphasizes only the sender and sending a message. It ignores the critical role played by the listener. So while consciously you are taught to think that communication is a two-way street, unconsciously it is strictly one-way.

Conduit metaphors convince your unconscious mind that communication involves the physical transfer of meanings, thoughts, and emotions from person to person. The only message that counts is the one that is sent. As far as the speaker is concerned, all the listener has to do is extract, or unpack, the thoughts from the words. It even assumes that the listener's definitions are the same as the speaker's. Regional differences,

"... in the future science will become more poetic. Our troubled world, too, is becoming too complex for logical argumentation, and may have to change its thinking: real trust, when emotions are running high, is based on analogy, not calculation.

> John J. Ratey,
> *A User's Guide to the Brain*, p. 5.

political implications, catchment words, and hot button inflections are ignored by the metaphor.

This philosophy reduces the listener's role to that of merely taking the intended meaning from the speaker's words.[6] We end up with very subtle expressions like, "It was hard to *get* the idea *across* to him." "It's difficult to *put* my ideas *into* words." "Your words sound *hollow*." "His words *carry* little meaning." "Try to *pack* more thought *into* fewer words." Subtle, yet very powerful to the unconscious.

The pervasiveness of metaphors greatly influences mediation parties' thinking and decision making. These metaphors, or mental frames, are part of their Hidden Area, in the synapses of their brains, physically present in the form of their neural circuitry. Scotomas hide primary metaphors that run counter to a party's perceptions. When the facts presented do not fit the frames, the *frames* remain and the *facts* are ignored.[7] If the information runs counter to the primary metaphor in their Unknown Area, they are literally unable to hear the perspective of the other side. Think of the child, when being told something she doesn't want to hear, who closes her eyes, puts her hands over her ears and says, "Nyah, nyah, nyah." Remember parties like that? Encouraging them to repeat the incongruent information out loud helps it break through their scotomas.

The way a conflict is metaphorically characterized also creates specific perceptions of what can happen, what will happen, what should happen, and what kinds of feeling actions might happen.[8] Metaphors casting a negative light on images and expressions stifle creativity. The parties' scotomas override their Reticular Activating System as it makes feeble attempts at broadening their thinking.

These perceptions and assumptions increase the importance of your role as a facilitator and interpreter between the parties. Reframing the conflict using positive metaphors, such as building a house, gardens, half-full glasses, and olive branches, can help crystallize a party's thinking. They help create alternative points of view as they compare the conflict to more productive objects or processes.[9]

The parties reveal themselves by the metaphors they use. Consider their statements and questions in terms of these conflicting metaphors. Your Reticular Activating System can then provide you with insights into the parties' deeply held

How the Conduit Metaphor Works

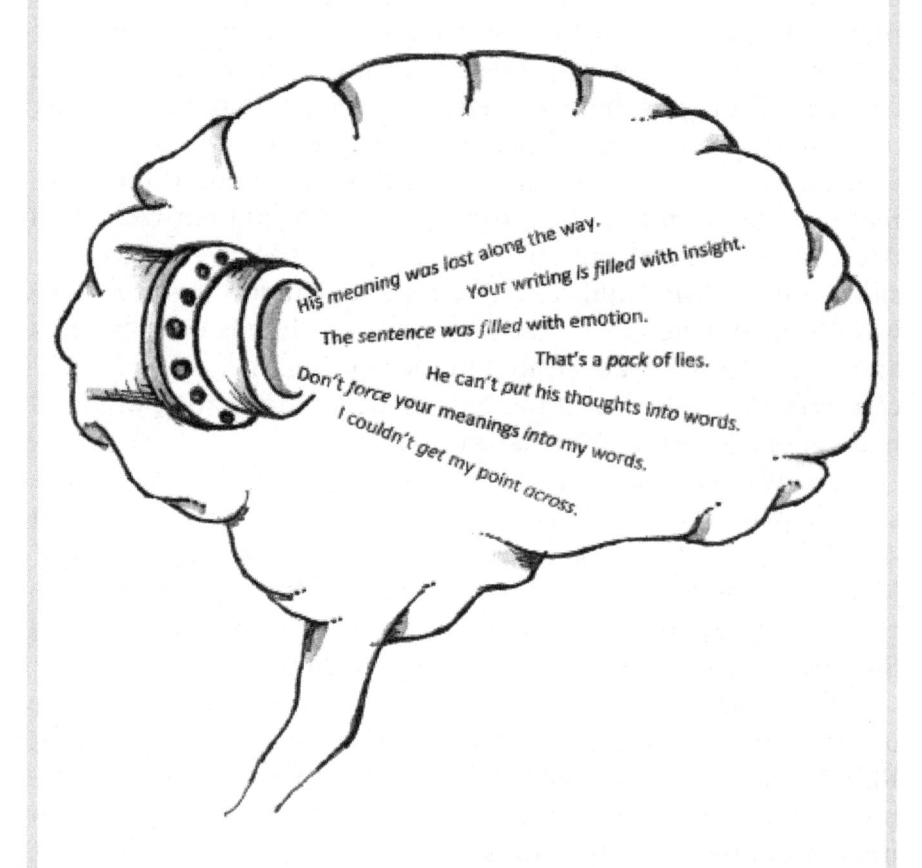

His meaning was lost along the way.
Your writing is filled with insight.
The sentence was filled with emotion.
That's a *pack* of lies.
He can't *put* his thoughts *into* words.
Don't *force* your meanings *into* my words.
I couldn't get my point across.

Adapted from George Lakoff,
Metaphors We Live By, pp. 10-13.

beliefs. Offering alternatives to their metaphors channels their perceptions towards a more positive, optimistic, and productive way of thinking. Sometimes just naming their metaphor and asking them to explain it to each other can help them get past their scotomas and perceptual blocks. For example, "What would it be like if the glass was half full?" or "When you say you are tilting at windmills are you saying you think the situation is futile?" Or, "Say more about the term "olive branch."

The conduit metaphor produces another problem in mediation. It inflates the speaker's confidence that their intended message is the message that is received, eliminating their need for repetition or redundancy. The parties assume that they can be successful without effort, reducing the amount of energy they are willing to devote to that effort. Ironically, the conduit metaphor takes successful communication for granted while, as you know, misperceptions and miscommunications are the most common causes of conflict. Yet those misperceptions are often among the last they seriously consider. Your task is to *unwrap* and *hand* clarity to the other party. Both parties need to be given the chance to *grasp* the other's meaning. Paraphrasing, restating, and reframing gives the speaker's meaning a better chance of being fully understood by the listener.

Primary metaphors inform a person's world view, causing people to place a higher priority on their values, their identity, and who they identify with, than they do on their own self-interests.[10] Their scotomas hide contrary mental frames that run counter to their perception, preventing them from seeing the incongruity involved. The Strict Father and Nurturing Parent[11] are two additional primary metaphors dominant in the U.S. today that can run counter to the parties' self interests.

STRICT FATHER METAPHOR

According to linguist George Lakoff, the Strict Father metaphor assumes that values are absolute and choices are clear. The world is and always will be a difficult and dangerous place. It is always competitive; there will always be winners and losers. In this model, children are born bad because they want to do what feels good rather than what is right. They have to be taught to be good. What is needed in this world view is a strong, strict father who protects the family from danger, has the moral authority to tell

The Strict Father Metaphor

A good, moral person is someone who is disciplined enough to be obedient, to learn what is right, do what is right and not do what is wrong, and to pursue her/his self-interest to prosper and become self-reliant. The Strict Father is the moral authority who has to support and defend the family, tell his wife what to do, and teach his kids right from wrong.

Assumptions:
- The world is a dangerous place because there is evil out there.
- Children are born bad and must be made good.
- The world is difficult because it is competitive.
- There will always be winners and losers.

Fear triggers the Strict Father model.

George Lakoff, *Moral Politics*, pp. 65-107.

his wife what to do, and teach his kids right from wrong.

The Strict Father metaphor also correlates morality with prosperity through self-interest. That means a good, moral person is someone who is disciplined enough to be obedient, has learned what is right, does what is right, and pursues her/his self-interest to prosper and become self-reliant. Most North American institutions promote and operate out of this primary metaphor, including school systems, the military, bank loan departments, insurance companies, and most Christian denominations.

The Strict Father metaphor is often evident in mediation sessions. The manager in the workplace mediation refused to promote the female employee to a position that allowed her to operate heavy equipment. That was men's work. She had run comparable equipment at her previous job and resented his refusal to allow her to earn the additional money the promotion represented. He did not see his position as discriminatory; he just wanted to protect her.

In another case, a custody mediation was stalled because of the stereotypes the parties had of each other based on their own primary metaphor. Ironically, both adhered to the Strict Father metaphor, but did not know it until they finally met face-to-face. The adoptive mother, Ann, was determined to raise her new baby to be a God-fearing adult. She assumed that the birth mother, Darlene, was an immoral, loose woman. On the other hand, Darlene was afraid she was giving up her child to a liberal do-gooder. Her worst fear was that Ann would be unwilling to give her son the proper religious instruction necessary for him to enter heaven.

Through much cajoling by the open adoption mediator, Ann and Darlene finally agreed to meet. As they talked they realized that they both held fast to the same primary metaphor. Ann could see Darlene as a fallen yet God-fearing woman determined to do the best for her baby. Darlene cried with relief to hear that Ann would provide her child with a proper religious upbringing.

Fear triggers the Strict Father metaphor, which often causes parties to invoke the metaphor during mediation. The metaphor's most important moral value is to preserve and defend the system itself. Since the entire model must be perpetuated, a party's adherence to this metaphor leaves little room for them to negotiate or compromise.

> Experienced mediators also know that they themselves respond differently to disputants in separate situations whose conflict dynamic appear similar. It is this factor that makes mediation a creative process.
>
> Michael D. Lang & Alison Taylor,
> *The Making of a Mediator*, p. 155.

NURTURING PARENT METAPHOR

In stark contrast, the Nurturing Parent metaphor embraces a very different world view. It assumes that the world is good and can be made a better place. The parent figure is gender neutral in this model. Both parents are responsible for raising their offspring, who are assumed to have been born good and able to be made better. Those who ascribe to the Nurturing Parent metaphor want their children to be happy and fulfilled, not just obedient. Therefore the parents feel responsible to be happy, fulfilled persons themselves.

Morality for the Nurturing Parent begins with empathy. Parents are empathetic, responsible people who protect and nurture their children and raise them to be nurturers of others. This hardwired metaphor assumes responsibility for the protection and the care of all individuals in the larger community who need care.

Those adhering to the Nurturing Parent metaphor want their children to be treated fairly, with dignity, and have the opportunity to prosper. The parents value open, honest, two-way communication. They believe in community-building, service, and cooperation because the community will affect how their children grow up. Fewer institutions ascribe to this metaphor, including Montessori Schools, Buddhists, and mediation programs.

Both the Strict Father and the Nurturing Parent mental frames include scotomas that mask input that runs counter to their core beliefs. This makes it difficult for the parties' to think creatively in areas affected by these conceptual metaphors.

America's politically conservative right and liberal left fall along the divide of these two metaphors. Conservative writer Thomas Sowell[12] asserts that U.S. democracy is divided by two dominant world views of mankind. Sowell labels them as "constricted" and "unconstructed," mirroring the Strict Father and Nurturing Parent metaphors. According to Lang and Taylor[13]

> ... both of these opposing views are valid, but they fuel the constant societal conflicts, because both are promoted in our society simultaneously. This schism of views may also apply to mediators. Those who believe that people have inherent tendencies toward evil, chaos, or negative behavior (the constricted view) might well try to exert control in the mediation process by creating rules and contingencies or by adopting a mediation model that relies on directive and controlling interventions. Mediators who hold the un-

The Nurturing Parent Metaphor

The Nurturing Parent values being empathetic, caring and responsible. Because they empathize with their child, they provide protection. They want their child to be fulfilled in life, to be a happy person. That means being trustworthy, honest, and fair. Open communication is fostered, as is freedom, opportunity, prosperity, cooperation and service.

Assumptions:

- Children are born good and can be made better.
- Both parents are responsible for raising the children.
- The world can be made a better place.
- It's the parent's job is to help that happen.
- The parent's job is to nurture children and raise them to be nurturers of others.

George Lakoff, *Moral Politics*, pp. 108-140.

constricted view and believe that disputants can be trusted to find their own solutions do not try either indirectly or directly to influence the disputants' decisions or to impose a solution on them. Deep core values, beliefs, and views necessarily influence to some degree all of a person's other theories, models, and facts, because all people tend to collect ... things that are part of a set, that are consistent with the other items in their collection of ideas.

As you might suspect, these metaphors have enormous implications for your impartiality as a mediator. If metaphors have such an unconscious effect on everyone, it follows that your own primary metaphors also unconsciously influence your ability to maintain a perceived impartiality. Your deeply-held beliefs cause your own scotomas. They influence your view of the world, keeping your unconscious Unknown Area closed. Becoming aware of these beliefs moves your Unknown line over, expanding your Open Area, and allowing you to monitor and control those beliefs within your conscious awareness.

Primary metaphors have an effect on all aspects of your life, also preventing you from entertaining certain creative ideas. For example, I find the menu for the Road Kill Café quite humorous when it sticks to Possum Stew and Raccoon Ratatouille. But, because all my dogs have been Retrievers, it ceases to be funny when it offers Chocolate Lab Cake.

It is also difficult for me to remain impartial in mediations where my own values run strongly counter to the values expressed by a party. While at the Better Business Bureau I declined to participate in mediations involving environmentally-damaging home chemicals. I did not even try to stay impartial toward someone who would allow chemicals to be applied at regular intervals where their children played. What mediation issues hit your values buttons?

As an avowed subscriber to the Nurturing Parent metaphor, I find it continually necessary to remind myself of the Strict Father metaphor's positive aspects. The following is the most extreme example of the chasm between the two metaphors I have experienced to date and its resulting challenge to my impartiality.

The veteran motorcycle patrol officer arrived precisely on time for the police/citizen mediation, long before the citizen, a third grade teacher, managed to find the meeting room. A month

Mediator Values:

- Being reasonable
- Good listeners
- Open-minded
- Respectful expression of our ideas

Norms We Often Promote:

- Separate the people from the problem
- Not ascribing motives to others
- Look for multiple options
- Use persuasion and interested-based approaches

> Adapted from Bernard Mayer,
> *Beyond Neutrality*, p. 124.

earlier he had stopped her for what was to him a routine traffic violation. She requested the mediation to express to him the extreme distress she felt by his behavior during the stop. She had been so traumatized by the stop that she had cried herself to sleep that night. She was there to convince him to change his intimidating behavior toward citizens at all his future traffic stops. As if ...

He explained it was his intention to be intimidating, that he never gave warning tickets, and believed in zero tolerance toward speeding. A person was either under or over the speed limit. Period. While he sat ramrod straight in his chair, I noticed his face redden as the veins in his neck bulged. He appeared to have to exert a great deal of effort to stay professional as she attempted to convince him to be nice while issuing citations. Her whole purpose in life was to teach children to be kind to each other. Couldn't he see the importance of that? It seemed as though she considered herself a failure if she could not convince that officer to see the world through her eyes.

I made futile attempts to find any commonality across the abyss that divided them. When the teacher had spoken her piece, the motorcycle officer responded that his methods had been effective for seventeen years and that he had no intention of changing them now. With that, he began re-layering his weatherproof garments. The teacher rushed from the room, no doubt to again cry herself to sleep.

Was I impartial? Hard to say. They were both caricatures of their respective paradigms. He was the stereotypical Strict Father; she was an over-the-top Nurturing Parent.

My impartiality was balanced only by being put off by both of them. When I start to feel that way, it is useful for me to think of severely Strict Father mediations as cross-cultural experiences, even when all the parties appear to be as mainstream Anglo as I am. Those are also the moments when it helps for me to remember Rumi's words, "Beyond the idea of right or wrong, there is a field, I will meet you there."[14]

Which of these two primary metaphors do you resonate with? Values mentioned in the mediation literature as important social norms include being reasonable and open-minded, being good listeners, and respectfully expressing opinions.[15] As described by Mayer and listed on pages 150 and 152, the norms promoted in

Values About Conflict
Include Certain Common Principles:

- Being hard on the problem, easy on the people
- Empowering disputants
- Respecting diversity
- Believing in communication
- Promoting social justice
- Valuing creativity
- Maintaining optimism

*Adapted from Bernard Mayer,
Beyond Neutrality, p. 124.*

mediation are all from the Nurturing Parent metaphor: separating the people from the problem, not ascribing motives to others, looking for multiple options, using persuasion and interest-based approaches.[16] The values Mayer[17] describes, empowering the disputants, respecting diversity, communication, social justice, creativity, and maintaining optimism, also fall within the Nurturing Parent metaphor.

ARMY VALUES

After a discussion of values in one of my mediation classes, a military veteran brought in her copy of the official Army Values,[18] listed on page 154. They all fall within the Strict Father metaphor. Since then I have always posted them on the wall during my mediation trainings. One time a mediation colleague came into the classroom, took one look at the chart, and stopped in his tracks with, "What's *this* about?" Their presence clearly was incongruent with his mediation values.

The Army Values encounter with the fellow mediator occurred just before I co-mediated an otherwise standard eviction case, one that vastly increased my understanding of the importance of primary values for resolving interpersonal conflicts.

During this particularly tough mediation, my co-mediator, Kevin Corcoran, said that it sounded like Dennis wanted to do the honorable thing. Suddenly something changed in Dennis' demeanor. Finally, after more than two hours of belligerence and hostility, Dennis began to engage in resolving the conflict. Here is the rest of the story.

Dennis and Tony were both forty-five year old tenants living in poorly constructed high-rise low-income housing. Tony, brain injured from a fall, lived directly above Dennis, an alcoholic, recently homeless Iraq War vet. The two had been at odds for months. Dennis hated the noise Tony made as he "slammed" his kitchen cabinet doors and constantly ground raw food for his macro-biotic diet. Dennis had verbally threatened Tony from time to time over the noise issues. Both men had sent letters to management trying to get the other evicted.

Kevin and I took a tag team approach. He took the lead for awhile, until Dennis made some scathing remark that left Kevin blank. Then I stepped in with a few questions until silenced when Dennis shouted, "That's irrelevant!" I shrugged and handed it

Army Values

Loyalty
Bear true faith and allegiance.

Duty
Fulfill your obligations.

Respect
Treat people as they should be treated.

Selfless Service
Put the welfare of others before your own.

Honor
Live up to these values.

Integrity
Do what's right, legally and morally.

Personal Courage
Face fear, danger or adversity.

The Seven Core Army Values, U.S. Army.

back to Kevin. It was about that time that Kevin mentioned the word "honor." Because Dennis had earlier referred to his Navy service, Kevin decided to give it a shot. It worked!

Within minutes they were discussing various ways Dennis could help Tony reduce the noise in his apartment. I took the risk of even injecting the Nurturing Parent word "community," which resonated with Tony. That also worked. They ended up agreeing on a joint shopping trip to buy felt pads for Tony's kitchen cabinet doors. Dennis volunteered to apply the higher pads because he knew Tony was afraid of heights since his fall. After they signed the agreement, Dennis ritually tore up his "evidence," stating that he would never use the complaint letters against Tony again.

During the debrief, Kevin told me that when Dennis mentioned he had been in the Navy, Kevin decided to try invoking military values, hoping Dennis would respond. "You sound as though you want to do the honorable thing," resonated both with Dennis' Army Values and the Strict Father metaphor. Dennis began to see Tony as someone he should protect rather than someone to guard against.

A week later, with tears in my eyes, I read a thank you note from Tony reporting that on the evening following the mediation the two of them had gone together to a Buddhist community gathering. Who would have thought?! From this mediation I learned that, regardless of which metaphor my mediation parties operate out of, if I can tap into the party's "frame," I have a mechanism for engaging otherwise entrenched parties in a more positive and productive manner.

I compiled the Values Inventory, found in the *Workbook*, by simply alphabetically listing Strict Father, Nurturing Parent, and Army Values. Which ones do you resonate with the most? More importantly, which one do you resonate with the least? When I distribute this as a survey during mediation workshops, I ask for a show of hands on the results. Mediators indicate a wide range of their most important values. When I ask about their least important choices, overwhelmingly their choices include Discipline, Obedience and Prosperity; all values from the Strict Father metaphor. Were any of these your least important?

Questions arise: Is the need to provide empowerment and recognition also part of the Nurturing Parent metaphor? Did you self-select to enter into the mediation profession out of your

When mediators know their constellation of theories and how it guides and informs their work, they are better able to integrate this knowledge during a session, and this integration of theory and practice contributes to their artistry.

> Michael D. Lang & Alison Taylor,
> *The Making of a Mediator*, p. 94.

belief in the Nurturing Parent metaphor? Regardless of which metaphor you adhere to, do you unconsciously attempt to impose your values onto the parties? Conversely, do the parties attempt to impose their values on you and/or the other parties? When either is the case, whose side are you on?

Think back on those mediations in which you had the most difficult time staying neutral. Which party just seemed more reasonable and easier to sympathize with? Which seemed less so? Being more consciously aware of your unconscious preference for either the Strict Father or Nurturing Parent metaphor moves both your Blind and Unknown Areas over toward Open. I find that it helps me to maintain my impartiality to acknowledge to myself that I am losing it.

To paraphrase the Sufi Master Hafiz,[19] with my italics added, "You have a *duty* to befriend those aspects of *obedience* that stand outside your house and shout to your reason, 'Oh please, Oh please, come out and play.'"

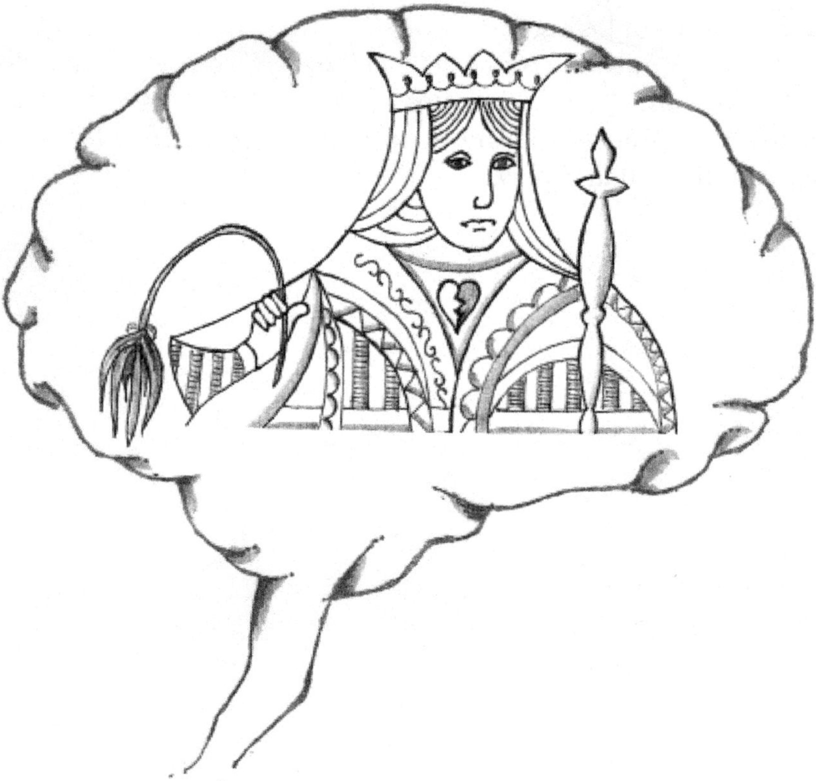

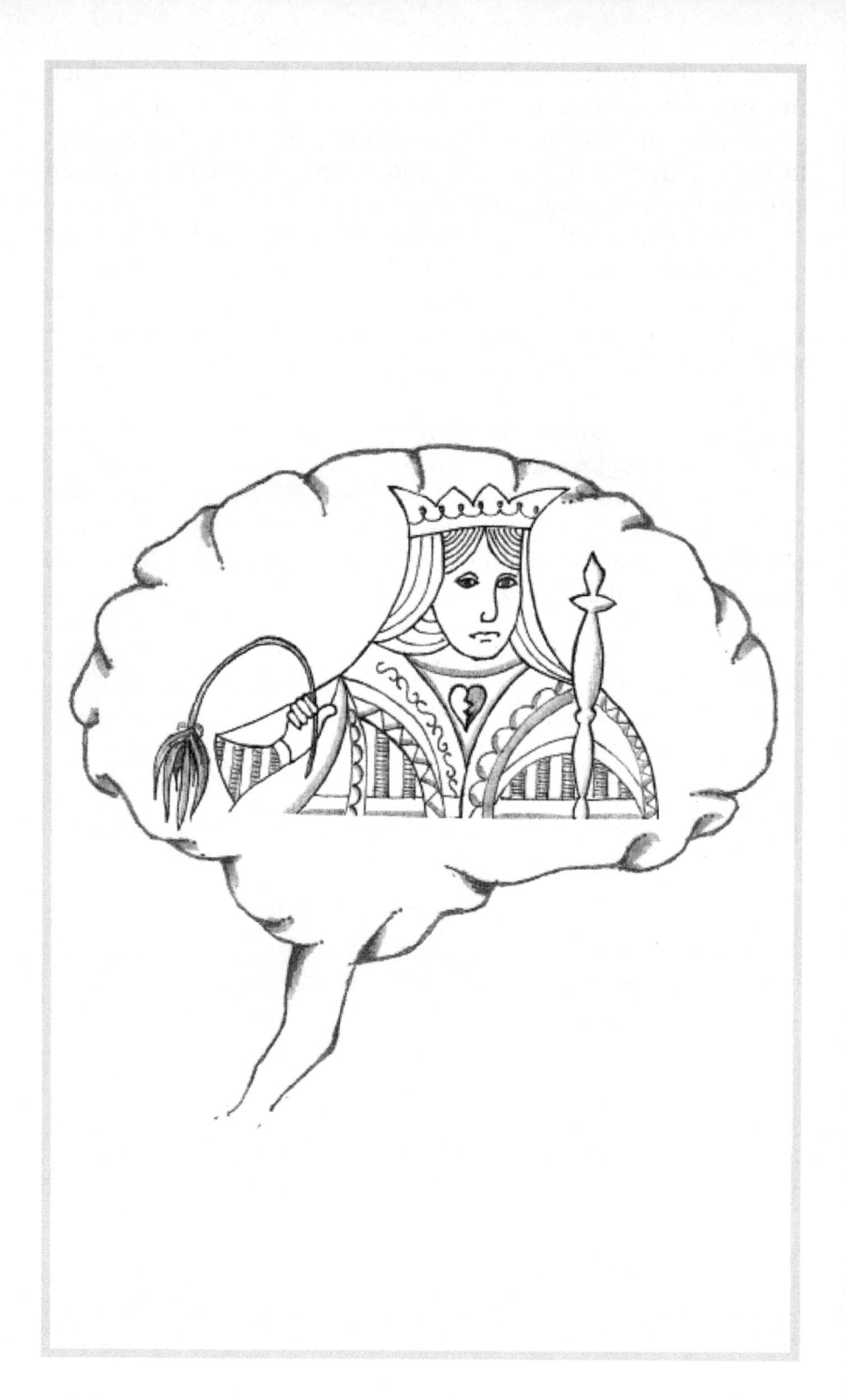

CHAPTER EIGHT

Picasso Meets the Red Queen

"Off with his head!" she said without even looking round.[1]

Think back to those mediations when things were definitely going sideways, when a party's unwillingness to mediate in good faith went far beyond their creative blocks. Was your mental balance thrown off, like a rug psychically being pulled out from under you? Did you physically react, becoming tense as your face flushed? Did you even have a flash of anger at the party? Did you feel caught, stuck, or pressured to respond in some way, by initiating, changing, or stopping the interaction?[2] If you answered yes to any of these questions, your Reticular Activating System was causing that voice in your head to shout, "Houston, we definitely have a problem."

Your party might very well have been a "Red Queen." Not being a psychologist, I am more comfortable using the character from Lewis Carroll's *Through the Looking-Glass* as a literary metaphor. The Red Queen character exemplifies those extremely difficult parties whose behaviors give every indication that they are not there to mediate in good faith. Instead, Red Queens (RQs) are there to attempt to exploit or manipulate you, the other party, and the entire process.

I don't have a magic bullet for you to use when dealing with a RQ. However, learning to recognize one keeps them from being able to blindside you and gives you the ability to protect the other party. You can also better protect the integrity of the mediation process by understanding the Red Queen's ability to manipulate and exploit it.

Some years ago a hospital human resources department brought me in as a long-term consultant to work on a difficult personnel situation. Tensions were high among the managers of the various medical units and departments. I worked directly

Red Queen Characteristics

Red Queens have a pattern of grandiosity, lack of empathy, and hypersensitivity to the evaluation of others. True Red Queens exhibit at least five of the following behaviors. They ...

1. react to criticisms with feelings of rage, shame, or humiliation.
2. are interpersonally exploitive.
3. have a grandiose sense of self-importance.
4. believe their problems are unique and can only be understood by other special people.
5. are preoccupied with fantasies of unlimited success, power, brilliance, beauty or ideal love.
6. have a sense of entitlement; an unreasonable expectation of especially favorable treatment.
7. require constant attention and admiration.
8. lack empathy; they are unable to recognize and experience how others feel.
9. are preoccupied with feelings of envy.

>Adapted from
>*Diagnostic and Statistical Manual of Mental Disorders,*
>p. 351.

with their new boss, Gwen. I had not been there long before the head of the psychiatric crisis department called me into his office and spent the next two hours of his day giving me a one-on-one tutorial on narcissistic personality disorder. In his professional opinion, Gwen was a classic case. It was so bad that he strongly felt that I needed this confidential background information to effectively work with her and her nurse managers.

Over the months that I coached and consulted with the nurse managers, at least ten of them individually presented me with materials on narcissism that they had researched for themselves or been given by their therapists. I had the diagnosis from the psychiatrist plus all these other assessments. By all accounts, Gwen was a clear-cut Red Queen.

Here is what I learned during my tutorial with the psychiatrist. According to *The Diagnostic and Statistical Manual of Mental Disorders*,[3] narcissism is considered a coping mechanism, not a mental illness. A personality is considered "disordered" when it is rigid to the point of being unable to change in reaction to changing circumstances. Personality distortions help narcissists resolve mental conflicts and the anxiety that usually accompanies those conflicts.[4]

Specific characteristics associated with narcissistic personality disorder are listed on page 160. Not all nine descriptors are always present in the same person. If you observe five of the nine, mix and match, you have a problem that will tax all your skills.

To varying degrees, Red Queens live in a fantasy of their own grandiosity based on their belief in their absolute perfection. They strive for constant attention and admiration. They are convinced that their problems are unique. These beliefs can combine in ways that cause them to feel envious and have a sense of entitlement, which when coupled with a lack of empathy can lead them to exploit others they consider vulnerable. Red Queens respond to perceived criticism with rage or by attempting to shame, humiliate, or intimidate others in their effort to end any challenge of their beliefs about themselves. Sound like any parties you may have dealt with?

Here is a snapshot of Mr. Pomeroy, an apparent RQ, who I once had as a party. He demanded the mediation and an apology from the police officer sitting across from him. The officer had dared to give him a traffic ticket, in spite of how special he

Alice ... explained, as well as she could, that she had lost her way.

"I don't know what you mean by your way," said the Queen: "all the ways about here belong to me—but why did you come out here at all?" she added in a kinder tone. "Curtsey while you're thinking what to say. It saves time."

Alice wondered a little at this, but she was too much in awe of the Queen to disbelieve it ...

> Lewis Carroll,
> *Through the Looking-Glass*, pp. 35-36.

was. After all, he was friends with the chief of police. Why, just last week he had lunch with his friend the mayor. How dare he be treated like a common citizen? Within that brief mediation I identified five of the descriptors shown on page 160 (numbers 1, 3, 4, 5, and 6).

Lewis Carroll's Red Queen embodies all nine of the characteristics associated with narcissistic personality disorder. After my tutorial with the psychiatrist I re-read *Through the Looking-Glass* with new understanding of Carroll's insights. I found quotes illustrating each of the nine RQ descriptors. After sharing my findings with a mediator and counselor friend, he confirmed that I had cracked Lewis Carroll's code.

Like Alice, everyone has experienced Red Queens, both male and female. Since my education on the subject and ongoing experience with Gwen and the nurse managers, I have shared information about Red Queens in many of my classes and consulting work.

Invariably, when conflict management students review the list of the nine descriptors, someone in the class recognizes a difficult person in their lives; such as their brother, sister, parent, neighbor, boss, or friend. Armed with new information, they are able to devise strategies for dealing with them. One student reported that now she just interviews her aging father when she visits him, rather than continuing to hope he will ever show interest in *her* life. Years after the class is over, I hear from students requesting a new copy of the materials because they had given theirs away to someone who needed the information. One man carried the descriptors in his pocket for weeks as he strategized ways to cope with his RQ business partner.

I include the information here for the same reason. It helped me cope with Gwen, overcome my unconscious blocks about my mother, and in the process become a better mediator. I believe it will help you deal with difficult clients in mediation, to say nothing of someone in your own personal or professional life.

Here is more of what I learned. Red Queens have several traits in common. A predominant characteristic is scapegoating. They become defensive at the slightest hint of criticism, disapproval or dissatisfaction with their performance.[5] They excel at crazy-making; causing others to have doubts about their own view of reality. They have perfected the double bind, so when dealing

Crazymakers are those personalities that create storm centers. They are often charismatic, frequently charming, highly inventive, and powerfully persuasive.

Crazymakers like drama. If they can swing it, they are the star. Everyone around them functions as support cast, picking up on their cues, their entrances and exits, from the crazymaker's (crazy) whims.

>> Julia Cameron, *The Artist's Way*, pp. 44-45.

with RQs you can end up feeling "damned if you do and damned if you don't." They need to keep others down in order to stay on top. You might hear something like, "Was John's presentation as bad as it was last week?"

Because Red Queens are so special in their *own* eyes, others can never be equal. Yet underneath their facade are feelings of emptiness, sadness, emotional absence, and meaninglessness.[6] Red Queens develop circular, ad-hoc, circumstantial, or even fantastic narratives to avoid confrontation with what they consider a disappointing and disillusioning reality.[7] In *People of the Lie*,[8] Scott Peck refers to narcissists as people who deliberately and consistently, over time, diminish the spirit of another.

> There are various essential attributes of life—particularly human life—such as sentience, mobility, awareness, growth, autonomy, will. It is possible to kill or attempt to kill one of these attributes without actually destroying the body. Thus we may 'break' a horse or even a child without harming a hair on its head.[8]

When I met with Edith, one of the more gruff hospital managers, I found her broken, beaten down, and distressed. Gwen had told her that none of the other managers liked her, and assigned Edith the task of interviewing them individually to find out directly *why* she was disliked. Amazingly pointless and cruel. I reminded Edith that conducting interviews like this were not in her job description and that she could just ignore the assignment. Gwen had so diminished Edith that it did not occur to her that she could refuse.

Peck considers narcissists "evil," which he defines as "using their power to destroy the spiritual growth of others in order to defend and preserve the integrity of their own sick selves."[9] Harsh words. Peck maintains Red Queens attack others instead of facing their own failure. They impose their will upon others by overt or covert coercion to avoid their own spiritual growth. Yet RQs are not "crazy." Like Gwen, they are coherent and self-possessed, they hold down responsible jobs, pay their bills, and function within the social system.[10]

Distrust was rampant among the hospital managers. Over time, several of them made appointments to have me meet them in their offices. When I arrived, they would often burst into tears, need assurance of my confidentiality, then share the latest of

Here the Red Queen began again. "Can you answer useful questions?" she said. "How is bread made?"

"I know that!" Alice cried eagerly. "You take some flour—"

"Where do you pick the flower?" the White Queen asked. "In a garden or in the hedges?"

"Well, it isn't picked at all," Alice explained: "it's ground—"

"How many acres of ground?" said the White Queen. "You mustn't leave out so many things ..."

>	Lewis Carroll,
>	*Through the Looking-Glass*, p. 171.

Gwen's imaginative methods for undermining their confidence. Midway through the meetings they again needed assurance of my confidentiality. After awhile, they would pull themselves together and I would leave after giving a third assurance of confidentiality. The next time I saw them in the hospital hallway, they gave no indication that they even knew me.

Yet, within her rigidity, Gwen was creative in her destructive manipulation. One way Gwen sowed distrust was by individually telling members of her staff that another staff member thought they were incompetent. I advised them to take the risk of calling the person in question directly and asking that individual if they had, in fact, said such things. Then one day Gwen announced to me that Sally, one of the managers, had told Gwen that she thought *I* was incompetent. I took my own advice and cautiously called Sally directly. Her response was, "Now she's doing it to you too!"

For awhile I attended their weekly management meetings. Then, one day Gwen, abruptly and without explanation, physically barred me from entering the meeting room. Yet I was allowed to continue, at regular intervals, presenting a variety of teambuilding workshops with the entire group. I soon developed two sets of plans for these sessions. One involved presenting standard off-the-shelf teambuilding exercises that I presented only if Gwen attended the session. If she was not there, the managers and I instead discussed how they were doing and strategized ways to survive another week of Gwen's abusive crazy-making.

Early on I attempted mediation between Gwen and the nurse managers. I realized too late that it was hopelessly doomed from the start. Although they had earlier voiced their willingness to meet, at the beginning of the meeting several of the managers were crying so hard that I rambled on with my opening statement for over twenty minutes to give them time to contain themselves. While in her own eyes she was the victim, Gwen had all the power in the room. No one really spoke out for fear of being fired. The impasse ended with everyone "making nice" and getting out of there. Over time, though, enough of us convinced upper management that Gwen was the central problem in the department so that she was finally persuaded to move on.

But there is one final kicker to this story. One of the managers became almost hysterical during my final private meeting

**Internal Strategies
for Confronting Red Queens:**
- First, check your intent.
- Stay focused on your point.
- Stop wishing the Red Queen were different.
- Be realistic about whether the potential Red Queen will change their attitude or behavior.
- Check your own reactions to the possible Red Queen.
- Monitor the effectiveness of your strategies.

**External Strategies
for Confronting Red Queens:**
- Keep control of the process.
- Be very directive if necessary.
- Deal with manipulation by directly naming the behavior.
- Short-circuit interruptions.
- Deal with extreme anger or emotion.
- Call for a caucus.
- Confront unacceptable behavior.

Adapted from Roger Fisher & Scott Brown, Getting Together: Building Relationships as We Negotiate, pp. 207-208.

with her. She confessed that Gwen had threatened to fire her if she did not agree to spy on me during the strategizing meetings when Gwen was not in attendance. Through her sobs, this single mother repeatedly apologized for her betrayal of the group. To keep her job she had been forced to compromise her integrity, her values, and her friends. Gwen had broken her without harming a hair on her head.

Granted, Gwen is an extreme case. My *Tales from the Hospital Crypt* illustrate the destructive nature of a real live Red Queen, who is still out there breaking other spirits.

Most Red Queens' behaviors and attitudes are isolated or intermittent enough to be only annoying. Although they sometimes are so annoying that they should be arrested. Think of the characters on *Seinfeld*. Or my least favorite character, Ray's mother on *Everybody Loves Raymond*. It is so well written that I can't stand to watch it. She is all too familiar to me.

In mediation, RQs are a problem when five or more of the nine descriptors are observable together as a pattern of ongoing behavior, like Mr. Pomeroy, the mayor's buddy. Once you understand the nine RQ descriptors, you can choose to either ignore them or to address them, depending on how much they prevent the possibility of a resolution, let alone reconciliation. The real difficulty comes when the RQ attempts to manipulate, intimidate, or shame *you*.

The Red Queens' creativity lays in their nimble ability to change the rules, the goalposts, or even the playing field in an effort to prevent someone from getting too close to discovering their inadequacies or deceptions. The situation intensifies if someone becomes a potential threat by becoming too competent. The RQ's ability to spin the facts, fabricate fantastic stories, and alter the rules or circumstances makes it very difficult to come to a durable agreement.

WHAT TO DO, WHAT TO DO?
You are well aware that as a mediator you are not trained or competent to diagnose mental illnesses or personality disorders. However, it is your responsibility to discern whether the parties are making a good faith effort to resolve the conflict. My intent here is to raise your awareness of the existence of Red Queens and offer creative strategies for responding.

"Now! Now!" cried the Queen. "Faster! Faster!" And they went so fast that at last they seemed to skim through the air,... till suddenly, just as Alice was getting quite exhausted, they stopped, and she found herself sitting on the ground, breathless and giddy ...

"I'm quite content to stay here—only I *am* so hot and thirsty!"

"I know what *you'd* like!" the Queen said good-naturedly, taking a little box out of her pocket. "Have a biscuit?"

Alice thought it would not be civil to say "No," though it wasn't at all what she wanted. So she took it, and ate it as well as she could: and it was very dry: and she thought she had never been so nearly choked in all her life ...

"Thirst quenched, I hope?" said the Queen.

> Lewis Carroll,
> *Through the Looking-Glass*, pp. 40-42.

These are the times when your Reticular Activating System or intuition starts asking questions like ...
Does this guy seem unusually angry, threatening or manipulative?
Does she seem to lack any empathy for concerns expressed by the other party?
Do they seem totally unrealistic about their responsibility for any of the dispute?[11]

Here are more questions for your RAS to have at the ready when you are on RQ alert.

1. *How well does your party empathetically understand the perceptions, values, interests, and motivations of the other party?*

> Young Henry had a job driving the beverage cart around a golf course. He was fired for stocking and selling beverages that he purchased on his own. He maintained that there is nothing in his job description that prohibited him from selling his own products. It didn't hurt the club's business. He explained that he was only providing golfers with drinks they couldn't get otherwise. It was simply a matter of supply and demand. Not only did Henry believe that he did nothing wrong, he instead insisted that he was being a "shrewd merchant." He resented being called a thief and demanded an apology from his boss.

2. *Do they tend to do and say things that weaken, undermine or sabotage the other party's ability to deal with them? Do they try to coerce the other party with anger, threats and/or warnings?*

> Amy wore thick, dark trifocal glasses. She was going blind in spite of three laser surgeries. Before she knew how serious her eye disease was, Amy had awarded the lone window desk to her subordinate and long-time friend, Rose. We were in mediation because Amy's doctor recommended she work by natural light, which made it necessary for her to be near the only window in the office. When Amy told Rose she would have to trade desks, Rose blew up and called her a "back-stabbing bitch!"

3. *Does the other party matter in their scheme of things?*

> Amy tried to give Rose the opportunity to voluntarily give up the window desk. She wanted to get back into Rose's good graces and be friends again. When I asked Rose

Alice was puzzled. "In *our* country," she remarked, "there's only one day at a time."

The Red Queen said, "That's a poor thin way of doing things. Now *here,* we mostly have days and nights two or three at a time, and sometimes in the winter we take as many as five nights together—for warmth, you know."

"Are five nights warmer than one night, then?" Alice ventured to ask.

"Five times as warm, of course."

"But they should be five times as *cold*, by the same rule."

"Just so!" cried the Red Queen. "Five times as warm, *and* five times as cold— just as I'm five times as rich as you are, *and* five times as clever!"

> Lewis Carroll,
> *Through the Looking-Glass*, p. 173.

if she understood the severity of Amy's condition, she responded, "Everybody's got problems," and went on to complain at length about her problems disciplining her teenage son.

4. *Do they give serious attention to the views, issues and interests of the other party? Do they put off, deflect or ignore the problems presented by the other party?*

Rose flatly stated that she did not believe Amy really was going blind. She demanded to see Amy's medical report, which Amy agreed to provide. Rose finally agreed to give up the window only when Amy agreed to give Rose an extra week of vacation.

5. *Do they seem reliable? Trustworthy? How much confidence can the other party have in their future conduct?*

At the non-profit board meeting I realized too late that the information I had just mentioned was not common knowledge among the group. My assumption was that if I was aware of it, others certainly had been similarly informed. Instead, a therapist on the board had unethically shared confidential information with me. I had to be silenced! She suddenly jumped up, loudly attacking me as "Goody Two Shoes" and "Dangerous to the group!" and that I "Must not be listened to!" We all sat back, stunned. Then someone asked, "Does anyone else think Louise is dangerous?" People looked at each other. "No," they said, shaking their heads in unison. The moment passed without further outbursts. Knowing what I know about Red Queens, I soon resigned from that board rather than again find myself in her crosshairs.

A LITTLE ADVICE

Once you begin to recognize the variety of RQ behaviors, you start to see how they work in combination. There are annoying garden variety Red Queens who only display a couple of the nine behaviors. But what can you do as you become aware of multiple and repeated patterns of negative behavior from RQs and other high conflict people? One obvious strategy is to privately raise your concern with them regarding their willingness to continue to make a good faith effort to participate in the mediation. (Ad-

Pay attention to the potential Red Queen's responses with these questions in mind:

1. How well do they empathetically understand the perceptions, values, interests, and motivations of the other party?
2. Does the other party matter in their scheme of things?
3. Do they give serious attention to the views, issues and interests of the other party?
4. Do they tend to do and say things that weaken, undermine or sabotage the other party's ability to deal with them?
5. Do they put off, deflect or ignore problems presented by the other party?
6. Do they try to coerce the other party with anger, threats and/or warnings?
7. How well do they seem to actually listen?
8. Do they seem reliable? Trustworthy?
9. How much confidence can the other party have in their future conduct?

> Adapted from Roger Fisher & Scott Brown, *Getting Together: Building Relationships as We Negotiate*, pp. 178-179.

ditional strategies are presented in Chapter Nine: Mediation as Improvisation.) Also, Bill Eddy's *High Conflict People in Legal Disputes*[12] offers in-depth strategies for dealing with Red Queens, along with borderline, antisocial, and histrionic personalities.

As mediator Jon Townsend says, "I know you didn't ask for my advice, so I'll be brief." The most important lesson I learned from Gwen and the other hospital managers I now pass along to you: avoid the naivety of thinking that your skills are going to level the playing field enough to neutralize the Red Queen's ability to wreak havoc on the other party's psyche. I have learned to be realistic about the probable Red Queen's desire or ability to change their attitude or behavior. It is not productive to be overly optimistic. Wishing "if only" is counterproductive and prevents you from dealing with the reality of the situation. In some cases you will have to guard the balance of power or even remove yourself from the mediation.

In extreme cases, if their responses confirm your suspicions, you may have to discontinue the mediation to maintain the integrity of the mediation process. Of course it is not always necessary to end it. There still might be a successful resolution of the dispute if you discern that the RQ has not manipulated the other party and if you are confident that both parties' needs have been met.

According to Peck there is evil out there in the world. It sometimes presents itself in a mediation session. RQs are practiced and accomplished at these negative behaviors, allowing them to totally overwhelm new mediators. Newbies can become confused and manipulated by the Red Queen's subtle maneuvering and control, as I was by Mildred during my first mediation. As Lang and Taylor state, "Mediators' responses to critical moments are often patterned and unconscious responses that show how they feel about themselves and their role."[13]

I always recommend that new mediators seek some form of professional therapy to deal with any past RQ issues causing creative blocks that may distort their ability to mediate. It sure helped me. Debriefing difficult mediations with experienced mediators also helps surface specific unresolved issues.

When presented with this Red Queen information, mediators have confessed their concern that they have some of these same traits. I have been asked, "Could it be that I'm a Red Queen?" If

> The Queen turned crimson with fury, and after glaring at her for a moment like a wild beast, began screaming. "Off with her head! Off ..."
>
> "Nonsense!" said Alice, very loudly and decidedly, and the Queen was silent.
>
> Lewis Carroll,
Alice's Adventures in Wonderland, p. 108.

you are asking yourself that same question, be assured that you are not a Red Queen because RQs do not ask that question! There is a difference between healthy narcissism, acknowledged competence and self-esteem, and unhealthy grandiose, manipulative self-absorption. Because they assume their own perfection and feel threatened by the topic, real Red Queens go on the offensive. A genuine Red Queen in the audience of my RQ workshops will argue with me, and even attempt to shame me for presenting this information. In contrast, "those who fully experience depression, doubt, confusion, and despair may be infinitely more healthy than those who are generally certain, complacent, and self-satisfied."[14] So relax ...

> Another aspect of congruence is the ability to behave in a manner that is appropriate for the particular clients we are serving. It is not that we as mediators fundamentally change who we are. It is rather that we accord our clients the respect of behaving in a manner that creates safety and inclusion for them as individuals, regardless of their background, appearance, or station in life.
>
> Daniel Bowling & David Hoffman, *Bringing Peace into the Room*, p. 28.

CHAPTER NINE

Mediation as Improvisation

"So, what's it like to be a mediator?"

How do you respond to that question? It is not as bad as it used to be when the idea of mediation was so foreign that people confused it with meditation, medication, mitigation, or referred to last night's mediator shower. So, in today's world, how do you best describe your role to those unfamiliar with the concept?

In books, mediators have been variously described as stage managers, directors, court jesters, and Coyote, the Native American trickster.[1] Like Coyote, you improvise to use your creativity to its maximum effect in the moment. Improvisational theater is an excellent way to invoke your trickster when a Picasso moment presents itself.

Like any other art form, improvisation needs to be practiced. Improvisation master Stephen Colbert[2] maintains that you improve your improvisational skills by simply remembering to say "*Yes, and*" in response to any given situation. As you read this excerpt from Colbert's 2006 Knox College commencement address, think back to your Picasso moments, when you creatively responded to what a situation threw at you. Then we will consider how you can be *more* deliberate about your own improvisations in the future.

> So, say "Yes." In fact, say "yes" as often as you can.... And yes-anding means that when you go on stage to improvise a scene with no script, you have no idea what's going to happen, maybe with someone you have never met before. To build a scene you have to accept. To build anything on stage, you have to accept what the other improvisers initiate on stage....
>
> You have to keep your eyes open to do this, you have to be aware of what the other performer is offering you, so that you can agree and add to it. And through these agree-

The trickster, like the mediator, crosses boundaries (both within and without), resides in boundaries, and stretches boundaries to uncharted territories. The mediator also requires creativity; a mediator must see issues in a new light and deliver them in a favorable package to the other party. Last but not least, the mediator is a peacemaker, using his or her inherent talent as a trickster, along with creativity and intuitive understanding, to bring peace into the lives of others.

Daniel Bowling & David Hoffman,
Bringing Peace into the Room, p. 7.

ments, you can improvise a scene or a one-act play. And because, by following each other's lead, neither of you are really in control, it's more of a mutual discovery than a solo invention. What happened in the scenes is often as much of a surprise to you as it is to the audience.

In mediation you also have to be aware of what the parties are "offering" you. Improv allows you to more freely respond to those offerings. One way to invite Picasso into the moment is to inhabit different personas. Consciously or not, you already assume different roles or personas just to maintain your perceived impartiality. Your own assortment of personas are probably conscious extensions of real roles you already play in your life; mother, father, sibling, boss, or teacher. Through improv you can "channel" these roles during mediations as the situation necessitates it. That is basically what you are doing when you invoke Peter Falk's TV detective character, Columbo, to clarify something a party seems to be trying to keep vague or obscure. "I'm confused ... a moment ago I heard you say X, now I hear you saying Y ..."

What other Trickster personas do you draw on when the situation demands it? Are you sometimes the Big Brother? The Trusted Friend? Advisor? Tough Negotiator? I have an assortment of personas I routinely use: the accommodating Little Sister, the assertive Substitute Teacher, the Literalist, and the Wall.

My most long-standing and reliable persona is Little Sister. During high school my older brother's friends usually hung out at our house. I wanted to hang out with them so I learned to be helpful, supportive, non-threatening, and just dang amiable. If I washed their hubcaps or cleaned their carburetors, they would let me go with them when they went out for hamburgers. I am comfortable and authentic in that role. When the parties are tentative, nervous, or at ease and productive, I settle into Little Sister; accommodating, impartial, and fairly invisible.

However, under more difficult circumstances I immediately invoke another available persona, the Substitute Teacher. I perfected my Substitute Teacher persona back in the days I was teaching those talented and gifted middle-schoolers. I can be cheerfully assertive, or not-so-cheerfully assertive. It is instantly available when I need to cut off shouting or other disrespectful behavior, intervene to preserve the dignity of the other party, or

> One of the most fascinating and powerful kinds of integral figures is the wise fool ... The fool's task is to undo complacency wherever he finds it ... He is the prince of paradox.
>
> We see him in the court jester, whose brazen buffoonery brings both challenge and release to the keepers of royal order ... we see him stepping blithely off the precipice of certainty ...
>
> > Charles Johnston,
> > *The Creative Imperative: Human Growth and Planetary Evolution*, pp. 286-287.

the integrity of the mediation process. The secret of my Substitute Teacher's success is that I only *momentarily* step outside of Little Sister to intervene. Once the party's behavior returns to within the agreed-upon guidelines, I instantly return to my Little Sister persona. When they step back, I step back, as if the incident never happened.

In one multi-party mediation, two seventy-year old parties, one a Mickey Rooney look alike, another resembling Charlton Heston, locked eyes as they loudly berated each other. Mickey then aggressively suggested that they "... take it outside!"

Fearing one would have a heart attack while the other broke a hip, my Substitute Teacher instantly shouted over their verbal jabs, "Hey!... (pause) Hey!... (pause) HEY!..." As my voice finally penetrated their focused concentration, they both turned toward me, stunned. I immediately lowered my voice and calmly interjected, "That's inappropriate." They sat back and regained their composure as I turned to the others, indicating for them to resume their discussion. That was the end of that.

Another of my personas, the Literalist, objectively takes people at their actual words, penetrating their values-based scotoma while coaxing them back into the process. The Literalist allows the listening party to hear the words which are really being said to them, "Actually, I heard her apologize to you." It also allows the speaking party to hear what they themselves have said: "You stated that you will never park there again. Is that accurate?"

I learned the Literalist persona at the elbow of Karen Hannan while working at the Better Business Bureau. During a mediation, George abruptly stood up to leave, announcing that he was "a good Christian and answered to a *Higher* Authority!" As George reached the door, Karen calmly replied that *we* only answered to the rules of the BBB. Amazingly, that seemed to satisfy George, who came back, sat down and resumed the mediation.

In another case, the city inspector had made an enemy of just about every other inspector at the mediation. He seemed impervious to their list of complaints about his behavior toward them. As I attempted to have him repeat back what had just been said to him, he spun around to me with, "What am I, a damn parrot?!" I responded to his manipulative behavior with an even, monotone Literalist voice. "Then you'd rather not repeat what he said?" The bonus was that it gave the others an opportunity to see

> Creative individuals are remarkable for their ability to adapt to almost any situation and to make do with whatever is at hand to reach their goals.
>
> Mihaly Csikszentmihalyi,
> *Creativity: Flow and the Psychology of Discovery and Invention*, p. 51.

a way to avoid being hooked by his shaming.

However, beware and be prepared for the worst. If the party turns out to be a Red Queen, these non-defensive responses to their manipulation may very well enrage them. The good news is that the other party will witness the RQ's rage or shaming being aimed at someone else. The situation presents you with the opportunity to model for them a different response to the intimidation.

My most memorable Literalist case involved Fred, who had threatened his neighbor with a baseball bat. At the beginning of the mediation he introduced himself with, "I was born an asshole, and then I got bigger." My intuitive sense was that Fred felt intimidated and needed to come on strong. He wanted to shock us, establish his authority over us, all while discounting the process. I momentarily pondered whether my Theory of Obnoxious People applied here. Namely, people who have been chronically demeaned tend to initially be obnoxious as a preemptive defensive maneuver. Being nice to them in the face of their obnoxious behavior models for them a different way of behaving. They might then risk being less obnoxious in return. With that in mind, my Literalist looked at him and calmly responded, "I appreciate your honesty." Then Little Sister stepped back in and continued the introductions. Fred did not get the reaction he expected. It worked. He ended the obnoxious behavior, stayed in the process and eventually even apologized to his neighbor.

Had I admonished Fred, the Designated Asshole, for being disrespectful, he would have had just the excuse he needed to get up and leave, having proven to himself and his wife that we were against him from the start. Had I ignored his comment the other party might have felt less safe and been less willing to participate. Instead, I chose in that moment to step into my Literalist persona, respond directly to his statement and honor his vulnerability without judgment. A Picasso moment if there ever was one.

Finally, I take on the impervious Wall persona when I perceive that a party is attempting to manipulate me, the other party, or the process by creating double binds, or otherwise shifting the goal post with a catch-22. These behaviors usually indicate that there may be a Red Queen involved. If so, it is usually necessary to meet them head on, sometimes without saying a word. Although

When I'm out of red, I use blue.

Pablo Picasso

ADAPT!

it is difficult and seems counter-intuitive, I stand my ground and momentarily morph into *Über*-Substitute Teacher: the Wall.

At the end of the mediation session, we were finalizing a date for a second session. An attorney for one of the parties suddenly turned to me and abruptly blurted, "Are you using mediation talk at us!?" An odd question to ask at that state of the proceedings. The date just selected by the parties interfered with his schedule. I assumed he was trying to assert his authority over me. Although he was sitting next to me, I did not give any indication that I even heard his comment. Instead, as the Wall, I concurred with the date that worked best for both parties and ended the session.

Some personas are best to avoid. People are more apt to have issues with Mother or Father personas than with Aunt or Uncle. The important thing is to use personas you already inhabit and can slip into and out of in a flash, such as Nice Neighbor, Mr. Rogers, or Yoga Instructor. Depending on the situation, the persona is friendly, helpful, definite, considerate, assertive, agreeable, and/or adamant. And, of course, always with a perceived impartiality.

An excellent time to assume a persona is when you are *not* feeling especially neutral or very compassionate toward a party. Think back to times you have initiated such persona-needed-here moments. Those times when internally you were screaming, "You did WHAT?!" while externally your tone and body language were impartially requesting them to, "Tell me more about that." The persona you intuitively picked allowed you to act "as if" you are neutral until you could return to your basic impartiality.

By altering your persona to fit specific situations you foster the parties' latent creativity and potential for empowerment as they problem-solve solutions and find avenues for reconciliation. Your improvised behavior was probably something you never learned in Mediation 101, but you knew intuitively and situationally that it was the appropriate action to take.

SITUATIONAL LEADERSHIP

Like improvisation, Situational Leadership is another contingency-based model that has intriguing implications for mediation. The basic tenets of the model provide a framework for empowerment that you can use as a means of meeting parties at their own stage of development.

To business guru Ken Blanchard,[3] "empowerment" means

Situational Leadership Model

SUPPORTING COACHING DELEGATING DIRECTING

Adapted from
Ken Blanchard, Patricia Zigarmi, & Drea Zigarmi,
Leadership and the One Minute Manager

accepting responsibility for your own actions, having a proprietary interest in the outcome of a situation, wanting to work hard for those results, all while feeling valued, involved, and proud of the work you do. He maintains that too many assume that "empowerment" means giving people the power to make decisions then giving them free rein to do whatever they want. Instead, his model offers a better understanding of what empowerment really is: releasing the power within people to achieve astonishing results. He maintains that while a key structural aspect of empowerment lies in giving people the authority and responsibility to make important decisions, it is not the whole picture, as some mistakenly think.

Blanchard characterizes leadership styles as the amount of *direction* and *support* given to followers. A situational leader analyzes peoples' needs and situations, and then adopts the most appropriate leadership style, or persona, to meet those needs.

As you see on the facing page, Situational Leadership divides leaders into four styles which, depending on the situation, call for the leader to be more or less supportive and/or directive.

DIRECTING LEADERSHIP
Directing leaders in business define roles and tasks, and closely supervise followers. Decisions are made, then announced. As a result, communication is largely one way. This correlates to the directive "settlement conference" model.

Regardless of the mediation model being used, the parties might lack the necessary confidence, specific skills or motivation required to participate in good faith. Those from The Strict Father metaphor might need more structure to feel that procedures are being properly followed. Some just behave badly and do not seem to be committed to the process or the outcome. They make it clear that they want to be absolutely right or to have their day in court. They threaten a law suit, yell at the other party, or are otherwise disruptive. My Substitute Teacher persona provides directive leadership for those who are resistant to mediation, for whatever reason.

The woman in mediation led me to believe that she was only there to support her recent-immigrant friend with limited English skills. As we were writing the agreement, the observer suddenly stood up and loudly interjected her own interests into

Empowerment

Releasing the power within people to achieve astonishing results:
- Accepting responsibility for your own actions.
- Having a proprietary interest in the outcome of a situation.
- Wanting to work hard for those results.
- Feeling valued, involved, and proud of the work you do.

Ken Blanchard, John Carlos, & Alan Randolph,
The 3 Keys to Empowerment: Release the Power within People for Astonishing Results

the discussion. When I told her the agreement was theirs alone, to finish on their own, she disclosed that actually she was her friend's realtor. She had a very vested interest in the outcome of the mediation. My very directive Substitute Teacher told her to wait in the hall. She stomped out of the room.

COACHING LEADERSHIP

Coaching leaders are still in charge, still define roles and tasks, but display more supportive behavior by seeking ideas and suggestions from followers. When applied to mediation, this style describes the opening statement. It also describes when agreements are being written; times that require you to be very specific, linear and task-driven.

For most parties this is their first mediation. Both the task and situation are new to them. They may have some relevant skills and display some competence, but they do not have the trust or experience to commit to an unknown process. The initial Coach persona provides initial high support and lots of structure so that the parties feel that they are in a positive, safe place. It is Little Sister with pom-poms.

Remember, neuroscience is finding that maintaining the 3:1 positive to negative ratio actually changes peoples' thinking. As mediators, we provide that ratio throughout mediations. It could contribute more to our success than anything else we do.

Another time for you to practice positivity in your Coach persona is when the parties' intense anger, stress and anxiety are personal blocks to their creativity. At these times, the party's brain function moves from their upper, frontal lobe area of logical thinking to their lower, limbic fight-or-flight thinking area. Women also respond to stress by attending to others. Scotomas kick in and they become "flat brained."

Pastor and councilor Jim Peterson describes flat brains this way. When someone is extremely stressed, a metaphorical balloon begins to inflate in their stomach.[4] This balloon then presses on their lungs, causing their breathing to become shallow. Next, the balloon presses on their heart so that they cannot express themselves. There is increased pressure on their ears and eyes so they cannot see or hear clearly. Finally the inflating balloon creates so much pressure that it flattens their brain and they can no longer *think*. This is not a good time to expect much creativity.

The basic idea is that when competence for a task (such as acting in an empowered fashion) is low, the leader ... needs to provide a great deal of directive behavior. As competence for the task increases, the amount of directive behavior needed decreases.

A similar relationship holds for commitment and supportive behavior. When commitment for the task is low (such as when someone becomes discouraged), the leader ... needs to provide a great deal of supportive behavior. As commitment for the task increases, the amount of supportive behavior needed decreases.

> Ken Blanchard, John Carlos, & Alan Randolph,
> *The 3 Keys to Empowerment: Release the Power within People for Astonishing Results*, pp. 24-25.

When your parties become flat brained in mediation, it is the time for your Coach persona to validate their feelings. Allow them to vent enough to reduce the pressure so they can breathe, speak, hear, see, and think again. Only then can they return to thinking creatively about their conflict.

Flat brains can be caused by immediate, acute situations or by huge, chronic problems. The parties become emotionally numb. Emotional numbness is usually associated with large catastrophes like floods, genocide, hurricanes, and earthquakes. But it can happen to parties because of difficulties in their lives, such as chronic medical problems, serious business downturns, or the loss of someone close to them. People reach this state when they have been overwhelmed with grimness, are suffering from compassion fatigue, or they just cannot take hearing any more bad news. When people who have been oppressed feel insecure or overwhelmed, feel they have "tried everything," they mentally shut down and quit even thinking about those things they consider hopeless. They become flat brained. They are certainly less able to process creative solutions. This is the time to be the supremely supportive Coach, radiating positivity.

Unless someone has had a successful background in dealing with conflicts they do not have a reservoir of confidence to tap into during new conflicts.[5] Unfortunately, if they have previously seen little difference between the expected outcome and the actual result, they can only sigh, "I'm wrong again." or "I can't do this." That becomes their brain's default message for dealing with any future conflict they will face. For them any problem appears unsolvable; out of reach. They may just want to give up before they ever get started. These are the times for your Coach persona to step up, pom-poms in hand, to build their confidence and consider that there might be a successful resolution of the current situation. Positivity is remarkably contagious. "People unconsciously mimic the emotional gestures and facial expressions of those around them."[6]

SUPPORTING LEADERSHIP
Supporting business leaders facilitate and take part in decisions, but their followers have control of day-to-day decisions such as task allocation and processes. In many mediations, a major portion of the session is spent in this quadrant. Support is high while

The Worried Flat Brain

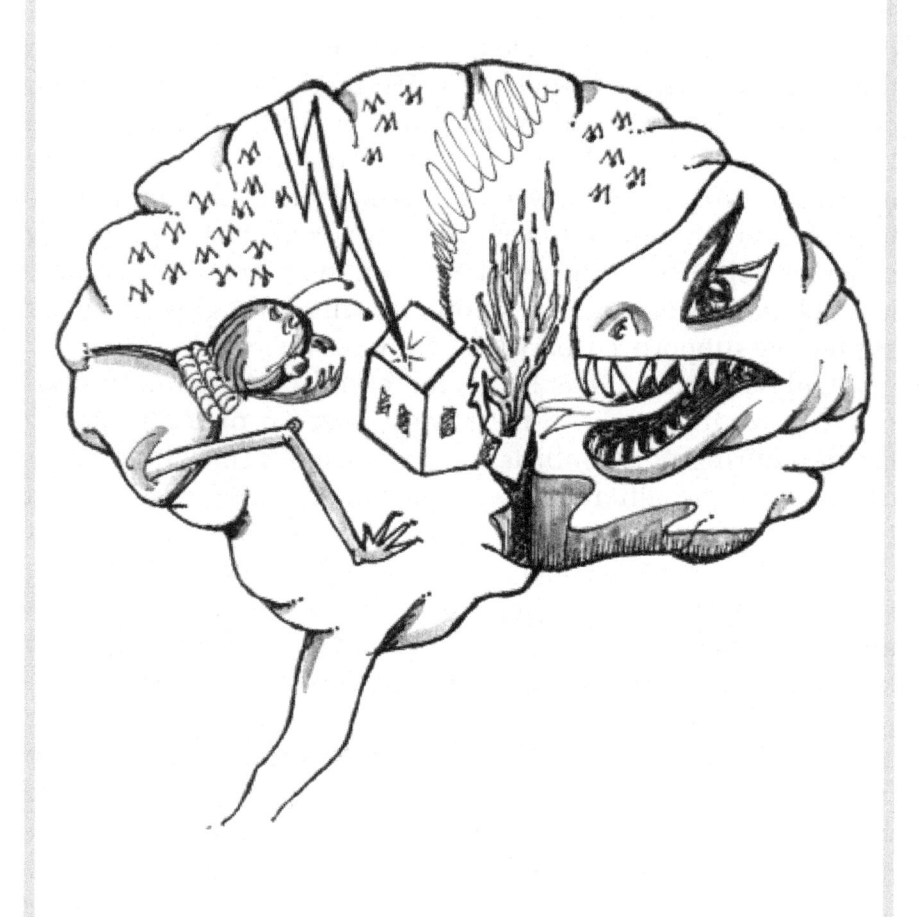

the need for directive behavior is limited. It is time for Little Substitute Teacher. Parties may be experienced and capable, yet may have creative barriers or just lack confidence. Their competence might be high, but maybe they are not totally committed to the process. In either situation they need more support to increase their confidence and commitment toward pursuing an acceptable resolution.

The workplace mediation was only scheduled to last an hour, hardly time for the two angry women to move from their tense distrust of each other to anything resembling reconciliation. As they realized that a third woman (from their description, perhaps a Red Queen) had been feeding both of them lies about the other, I interjected with the question, "Since we agree that this needs to be a speed mediation, would either of you mind if I put forth an idea that might help the situation?" With their permission I asked what would happen if they had very public weekly lunches together in the work cafeteria? They immediately got the point and began scheduling their lunch dates, recognizing that being seen together would negate the power of the troublemaker.

DELEGATING LEADERSHIP
Delegating business leaders are still involved in decisions and problem solving, but control is with the followers or parties who engage in their own conversation and decide when and how the leader will be involved. This style is the ideal mediation scenario; the parties are autonomous, competent, empowered, and reasonable. They are willing to listen to and hear each other. They are problem-solving ways to resolve their own dispute. These are parties who are calm, confident, and/or experienced with mediation, very knowledgeable about the process, and/or are very comfortable with their own ability. They display high competence and high commitment. When this is the case, after the obligatory opening statement, I silently settle back into my Little Sister delegating mode and let them take care of their own business.

Although the citizen, an attorney, had requested the mediation with the police officer, he refused to sign the agreement to mediate. I explained that I could not go forward without it. The officer was so anxious to tell his own story that neither got up to leave. I suggested they go across the street to Starbucks to talk. No movement. Silence. Then the officer blurted an apology for

> Many more of us are naturally confused, voyeuristic, compulsive, and marginal than we're rational, patient, and understanding in the path of conflict. The difference is that a sophisticated natural mediator has learned not to deny his or her basic nature, but rather to harness and use those amply provided attributes or vulnerabilities to our advantage.
>
> > Robert Benjamin,
> > in *Bringing Peace into the Room*, pp. 87-88.

the mix up that got them there in the first place and began his lengthy story of having been falsely accused himself. I remained silent and motionless for an hour and a half as they each replayed the precipitating incident from their own perspectives. Then they philosophized about the nature of guilt and innocence in the U.S. judicial system. When they were talked out, the attorney thanked the officer for his time. They shook hands and left the room. I quietly witnessed recognition, empowerment, and transformation, all without benefit of an opening statement or confidentiality agreement, with just Little Sister sitting by.

Just as the Situational Leadership Model is a key to business success, it can also be a useful frame of reference for successful mediator behavior. Like your creative styles, personality types, and conflict mode preferences, you tend to have a preferred "situational mediation" style. For those of you who are attorneys with a strong preference for a more evaluative settlement conference, this model offers a method for considering ways to flex into an appropriate persona when you want to be more supportive. For those of you with a strong preference for non-directive and accommodating facilitative styles, it provides a framework for considering when and how to be more directive to meet the parties' needs.

The model works across cultural, language, and geographical barriers.[7] It presents another way to diagnose the needs of the parties at a particular point in time and to use the leadership style and persona that matches and responds to the needs of the situation.

> Knowledge of the creative process cannot substitute for creativity, but it can save us from giving up on creativity when the challenge seems too intimidating.
>
> Stephen Nachmanovitch, *Free Play*, p. 12.

CHAPTER TEN

In Defense of Creative Problem Solving

In Chapter One I mentioned that there might be times when you find yourself resistant to new ideas presented here. This might be one of them.

The field of mediation itself has produced another subtle, yet very real, block to your creativity. The field has evolved into "several distinct groups of practitioners who sometimes seem to speak different languages in describing the techniques, styles, models, processes, and desired outcomes of their work."[1] A lack of understanding of the term "problem solving" has contributed to that block.

Problem solving is another of those catchment phrases whose shared definition is taken for granted, leading to assumptions and misinformation. In the field of mediation "problem solving" has been inaccurately assumed to imply that you are evaluating, advising, or otherwise telling the parties what to do. It has been assumed that problem solving equals advice-giving and is therefore from hell.

Reading *The Promise of Mediation*[2] was a very frustrating experience for me. Problem solving was constantly dismissed as bad, yet I never once found a definition of it. And, believe me, I looked. Having extensively studied problem solving in graduate school, I felt as if I was constantly seeing my name misspelled.

A few years ago I attempted to correct this misperception by presenting an Oregon Mediation Association Conference workshop titled, "The Naked Truth About Problem Solving." I wanted to set the record straight, at least where demonizing problem solving was concerned. I even brought along a soap box to stand on while ranting into the wilderness that transformation is an outcome, not a process. Any transformation in thinking involves the creative process! Participants in my Naked Truth Workshop sure

Creative Problem Solving is a comprehensive ... system built on your natural creative processes that deliberately ignites creative thinking ... It also encompasses everything involved in looking for or refining those answers ... CPS as a process is about transforming creative ideas into creative solutions for complex problems ...

CPS is useful in dealing with predicaments and opportunities ... through deliberate application of the creative process.

> Gerard Puccio, Mary Murdock, & Marie Mance, *Creative Leadership: Skills That Drive Change*, pp. 29-34.

heard an earful, including that the "directiveness associated with problem-solving mediation" that Bush and Folger[3] warn against only happens in settlement conferences conducted by attorneys, judges, law clerks, law students, or other members of the legal mediation community. Those of you who mediate workplace, community/neighborhood, small claims, landlord/tenant, and other non-legal disputes, are not involved in evaluative, directive, settlement-oriented legal mediations, or settlement conferences.

Continuing my rant, I further noted that directive "problem solving," when it does occur, is not to be confused with the Creative Problem Solving: Thinking Skills Model, which even uses "transformation" in its definition:[4]

> ... a comprehensive cognitive and affective system built on our natural creative processes that deliberately ignites creative thinking and, as a result, generates creative solutions and change ... Transformation begins with the broad search for potential ideas to address previously identified challenges ... and ends with the best ideas being developed into concrete solutions.

From my soap box I emphasized that creative thinking is needed *whenever* there is something wrong with an existing situation and the old remedy no longer corrects it. With both predicaments and opportunities, solutions are unknown and need to be discovered through the deliberate application of the creative process.[5]

The phrase "creative process" refers to a sequence of steps or stages you engage in when clarifying a problem, working with it to produce a solution that resolves a difficulty. It refers to the relatively rapid perceptual change or transformation that takes place when a new idea or problem solution is suddenly produced or detected. Finally, the creative process refers to the techniques and strategies that you use, sometimes consciously and sometimes unconsciously, to produce the new idea combinations, relationships, meanings, perceptions and transformations.[6]

Various creative processes offer a range of tools, from practical nuts-and-bolts approaches to a heavy reliance on the participants' imagination. The Kepner-Tregoe Model[7] uses deductive reasoning to discover a single predetermined correct answer, like a mechanical failure or whodunit. Think Sherlock Holmes. At the other extreme, the Synectics Model[8] is used to solve not yet

Creative Problem Solving: Thinking Skills Model

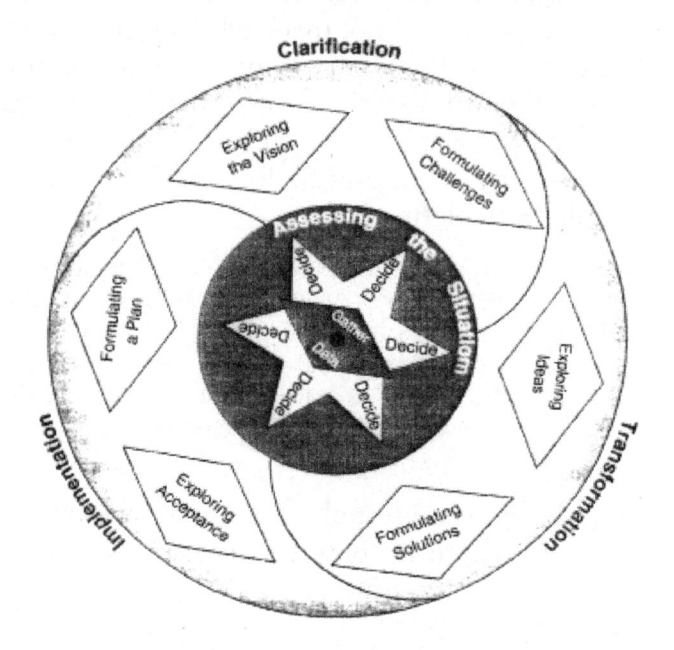

Clarification: To get started with any process, you must understand what needs to be solved.

Transformation: Next, you need to identify potential ideas and craft them into workable solutions.

Implementation: Finally, you need to refine the solutions and put together a plan for taking effective action.

> Gerard Puccio, Mary Murdock, & Marie Mance, *Creative Leadership: Skills That Drive Change*, p. 34. Used with permission.

existing, future-based problems, including product innovation. Synectics' operating principle is to make "the familiar strange and the strange familiar." Synectics incorporates metaphors that jog your Reticular Activating System into making new connections to previously unrealized possibilities. ATM machines were first contemplated using a cactus metaphor: something difficult to get into yet containing something of value inside. And Velcro was envisioned from cockleburs hitchhiking on socks.[9]

The original Creative Problem Solving (CPS) Model moved between the extremes of these other two, encouraging an infinite number of possibilities yet fostering solutions realistic enough to be implemented. The CPS Thinking Skills Model evolved from the earlier, more linear model. Its circular format acknowledges the cyclical nature of life.

As you can see on page 202, within this cognitive model there are three major regions or stages: Clarification, Transformation, and Implementation. They follow explicit process steps, with repetitions of idea generation and decision making occurring in each one.

The initial Clarification Stage of the CPS Thinking Skills Model is like story telling in mediation; the problem is introduced, giving the parties/clients an understanding of what needs to be solved. Participants are asked to consider current challenges or opportunities in their own life by asking themselves, "Wouldn't it be nice if ..." This open-ended question sends their Reticular Activating System into high gear. Over the years the top three challenges for my workshop participants have always been, "Wouldn't it be nice if I could lose weight ... quit smoking ... manage my time better ..." What have been your consistent challenges over the years?

In the second phase, called the Transformational Stage, participants in the workshop join Resource Groups where potential ideas are identified, nurtured, and elaborated upon. The Resource Group's expressed purpose is to be deliberately creative by applying specific methods and techniques to a concern or potential opportunity raised by a "client." A recorder is selected for each person. In one workshop, when it was her turn to be the client, a single mother read her "problem statement" and briefly gave some background information. Then others in the group brainstormed possible solutions for her. "Clients" can contrib-

CHAPTER TEN—IN DEFENSE OF CREATIVE PROBLEM SOLVING | 203

Mediation as a Giant Puzzle

Stage One is the puzzle box itself, opened as the parties review goals and purpose of mediation, and agree on guidelines.

Stage Two involves dumping out all the pieces to get a general picture of the problem, organize and prioritize an agenda. Slowly working on different sections helps the bigger picture come alive.

In **Stage Three**, discovering corners of puzzle, provides a coherent framework to reduce anxiety ... the real work starts here.

In **Stage Four** chaotic puzzle images transition closer to completion. Everyone is working on puzzle with the intent of finishing it.

By **Stage Five** pieces are all used, puzzle is completed. Or a few missing pieces are yet to be found.

>Olivia Yeung,
>*personal communication, October 23, 2008.*

ute their own ideas, but are not allowed to shoot down others' ideas. Ideas are put forth in the form of questions that start with "In what ways might you ...?" Someone in the mom's Resource Group asked, "In what ways might you involve your ex-husband in strategizing about your son?" This idea came as a Blinding Flash of the Obvious to the rest of the group, but the mom had never even considered including her former husband!

In the final, Implementation Stage, solutions are refined and structured into a plan for effective action. The single mom left the workshop with new insights and a solid Plan of Action to allow her ex-husband to be more present in their son's life.

People in the workshop were amazed at the number and variety of ideas others generated for them. The ideas considered most viable were further refined into workable solutions by the clients. Nobody gave advice or otherwise told them what to do or how to do it. Through this workshop experience they understood The Naked Truth About Problem Solving. And now, so do you.

Another Blinding Flash of the Obvious I had years ago is that, on paper, mediation and Creative Problem Solving are virtually identical. This was repeatedly driven home to me as I taught CPS to the gifted middle school kids in the morning and studied mediation in the afternoon. As you can see from the chart on page 206, mediation and CPS have several specific features in common. With both processes, mediators and CPS facilitators ...

- are trained to remain neutral and ask open-ended questions.
- initially give participants information about the process.
- attempt to make participants feel comfortable.
- refrain from entering into the content the parties or clients have brought to the session.
- have defined stages that the facilitators and mediators trust and rely on.
- have stringent rules for participants' behavior, which are explained and enforced by the facilitator, assuring that all ideas will be accepted.
- discover the interests of the parties.
- offer the opportunity for people to achieve greater under-

Similarities and Differences Between Mediation and Creative Problem Solving

	Mediation	CPS
Neutral Facilitation	X	X
Defined Stages	X	X
Guidelines	X	X
Ideas Strengths/Weaknesses Discussed	X	X
Client is Decision-Maker	X	X
Written Agreement/Plan of action	X	X
Determine Criteria for Decision-Making	X	X
Confidentiality	X	
Membership in Sanctioning Organization	X	
Assumed Conflict	X	
Informal Group Brainstorming	X	
Formal Group Brainstorming		X
Resource Group		X

standing of their own, and each other's, options.
- begin with an initial stage which emphasizes that all decision making is left up to the clients.
- offer the potential for next steps after the session is over.

There are opportunities within both processes for everyone attending to present their own thoughts. In both processes decision making is very deliberate. After a range of criteria is carefully considered only the client decides what ideas to keep and build on. In both, there is the opportunity for a written agreement, aka Plan of Action. As in mediation, a Creative Problem Solving (CPS) facilitator is at the heart of the model to guide them all.[10]

As you can also see on the chart, there are essential differences between the two processes. During facilitated CPS sessions the assumption is made that everyone in the Resource Group is on the same side. Unlike mediation, there are no specific provisions for potential conflicts. On the other hand, both processes emphasize the need for idea generation as a means of finding viable solutions to a problem. Standard mediation training does not provide much guidance on how to help parties envision new solutions to their disputes. Creative Problem Solving does.

As part of any Creative Problem Solving or basic creativity workshop or seminar, I always discuss the concept of divergent and convergent thinking. Divergent refers to the expansive, no holds barred—dare I say—right-brained kind of thinking we associate with brainstorming. Convergent thinking is the opposite. It is the judging, discerning kind of critical thinking required to bring ideas back to earth.

In seminars I rely on the familiar car metaphor to explain divergent and convergent thinking. To get anywhere you cannot have one foot on the brake pedal while the other is gunning the engine. It is an easy metaphor because creative thinking operates the same way. Its success depends on the dynamic balance between the gas pedal—divergent thinking (idea generation) and the brake pedal—convergent thinking (decision making).

DIVERGENT THINKING GUIDELINES—WHEN GENERATING IDEAS
Divergent thinking (idea generation) leads away from a preferred or agreed-upon solution by incorporating fluency, flexibility, originality, and elaborative thinking. As you recall, fluency is the

CHAPTER TEN—IN DEFENSE OF CREATIVE PROBLEM SOLVING | 207

> ... people will naturally move forward, backward, and across these elements ... So, although the three stages of CPS represent the natural progression individuals go through when faced with an open-ended problem, this flow will not always occur in a sequential manner. Sometimes it may seem like you have skipped stages, but in reality your mind is working so quickly that you may not be aware of your stages of thought, or the issue may be relatively simple and require less time to process.
>
> Gerard Puccio, Mary Murdock, & Marie Mance, *Creative Leadership: Skills That Drive Change*, p. 36.

ability to generate a great quantity of ideas. Flexibility means switching from one perspective or category to another. Originality involves generating unusual associations of ideas. Elaboration refers to the amount of detail included in any of the ideas generated.

Creativity does not mean anarchy. Everything has its boundaries and there are always constraints involved. Creative Problem Solving is no different. There are six ground rules explained and enforced by the facilitator.[11] As you read the following idea generation guidelines, think of how they apply to mediation. Let your Reticular Activating System remember examples from mediations you have been involved in.

- **Defer judgment** is CPS terminology for what the mediation field calls neutrality or perceived impartiality. It is why CPS facilitators respond, "Say more about that," instead of, "That's never going to work!" Both processes advocate active listening and suspending your own sense of what the solution should be.

- **Look for lots of ideas** encourages both sides of a dispute to consider new options and solutions generated by the other side. Some in the mediation community maintain that the mediator should not, under any circumstances, offer ideas to the parties. However, it is possible to indirectly ask a carefully considered open-ended umbrella question in a way that keeps the parties in control over the content of their own mediation. For example, "What are some ways you could follow the judge's order on supervised visitations …?" or "In what ways might you allow your daughter to see her dad and still have everyone be safe …?"

  Another technique is to ask the parties' permission to offer solutions you know others in similar situations have agreed to. For example, "I remember mediating a situation with issues very similar to yours. They came up with a unique resolution that might be useful here. May I share it with you?" This is not to be confused with giving advice, as in, "Here's what I think you should do."

- **Accept all ideas** correlates with mediation's instructions to include both parties' issues as well as their ideas for

Idea Generating Guidelines

Defer judgment
Look for lots of ideas
Accept all ideas
Let ideas "simmer"
Make yourself (and the parties) "stretch"
Seek combinations of ideas

> Scott Isaksen & Donald Treffinger,
> *Creative Problem Solving: The Basic Course*,
> pp. 2-5–2-7.

resolving them. By writing down all ideas you are noting potential solutions so they are not forgotten later. You have seen how sometimes a party needs to ponder an idea before accepting it. That idea may be the unexpected solution that they were unable to consider earlier.

- **Let ideas simmer** when parties have reached an impasse. As you know, sometimes a party needs time to mentally strategize, get past their scotomas, or just come to terms with accepting a potential solution. This is especially true when it was not their idea. Introverted and perceiving parties may need more time to reflect on an idea before committing to it. You know when to encourage a break, or to just change the subject and then revisit the idea later.

- **Make the parties 'stretch'** by asking them if they can think of any other, outside the box ideas. You can mention other hypothetical options, even labeling them as "wild and crazy." When one party's initial ideas are totally rejected by the other side, you can assume the Agent of Reality or Prophet of Doom persona to point out the obvious. When party A says, "I want to never see my co-worker again!" your response can be, "Since you have no control over that, can you think of solutions that you do have control over?"

- **Seeking combinations of ideas** is called "packaging" by negotiation experts.[12] Asking lots of hypothetical questions encourages the parties' Reticular Activating Systems to consider new combinations. For example, "If they are willing to do ABC, would you agree to XYZ? What about A, B and H?"

CONVERGENT GUIDELINES—WHEN MAKING DECISIONS

Because idea generation is the only kind of thinking measured by most creativity tests, we usually do not consider decision making as creative. But the convergent, decision making aspect of creativity is just as essential as idea generation. We need the brake pedal. The convergent guidelines facilitate the parties' ability to come to an intuitive knowing of viable potential solutions that can ultimately be accepted as part of a mediated agreement.

You may be surprised by the convergent (decision making)

Advocates need to be creative problem solvers. This means being able to see their way through to a substantive solution of a client's problem. It may also involve being creative about strategy, tactics, and intermediate problems that clients face in carrying out a conflict. A good solution to a conflict requires creative problem-solving ability.

Bernard Mayer, *Beyond Neutrality*, p. 256.

guidelines.[13] They are another place where Creative Problem Solving process and mediation processes intersect. They are both designed to achieve the same purpose.

- **Be deliberate.** When you methodically probe into each of the parties' agenda items, issues, and interests you are following this creativity guideline. You revisit, and then build on, issues previously agreed upon, taking time to validate previous agreements and reinforce positive stances. To reach a durable agreement you are willing to wade into issues you fear will upset a party or otherwise reignite hostilities. Throughout the mediation, you check for the parties' understanding of words, phrases, and concepts. Sometimes you are blunt, "A moment ago Kelly said he really wants this to work out. Do you believe him?"

- **Be explicit.** This is especially necessary when establishing the mediation guidelines during the opening statement and while writing an agreement. You repeat back potential catchment words, misunderstood references, or semantics that may unwittingly contribute to prolonging the conflict.

- **Avoid premature closure.** You ask the parties about their deadlines and timelines, or why they seem to be in a hurry to end the mediation. You are cautious to resist parties' desire to rush to judgment or agreement. You protect the integrity of the process, even when one of the parties wants to push through to a quick solution. Instead, you take the time necessary to explore all the options presented.

- **Look at difficult issues.** This is, of course, why the parties are mediating in the first place. You make a deliberate effort to anticipate difficulties that might not be obvious, but might nevertheless influence the parties' decisions. New mediators are often afraid to wade into the turbulent waters of what has already been expressed as entrenched, positional, or absolute. But you know it has to be done if there is to be any hope of resolution or reconciliation. The solution always resides within the conflict. It can only be found by probing those areas that are most conflicted.

Decision Making Guidelines

Be deliberate
Be explicit
Avoid premature closure
Look at difficult issues
Keep your eye on your objective
Develop Affirmative Judgment

> Scott Isaksen & Donald Treffinger,
> *Creative Problem Solving: The Basic Course*,
> pp. 2-7–2-8.

- **Keep your eyes on your objective.** Adhere to a tested process. The agenda items are a means of methodically determining each of the parties' issues and interests. When the parties go off on a tangent, you draw them back as you keep probing for possible areas of agreement, resolution and reconciliation. You focus on the concerns that are most important to the parties. Most of all, you trust the process.

- **Practice "affirmative judgment."** You rely on your positivity to maintain an optimistic attitude throughout, which raises the parties' positive to negative ratio. When the parties' present an idea for a possible solution, it is essential to first invite them to consider what might be the advantages of the idea before delving into its limitations. Doing so keeps their Reticular Activating Systems open to new possibilities and encourages them to stretch, look at all ideas, and avoid premature closure.

CPS/MEDIATION HYBRID

Here is a brief case study of a hybrid approach that explicitly incorporated Creative Problem Solving in mediation. Most mediators already use some type of hybrid approach to mediation; combinations of facilitative, transformative and evaluative approaches.[14] How often have you found yourself in situations where you have had to create hybrid roles; mixtures of more defined and established roles, such as mediator/arbitrator, therapeutic mediator, trainer/facilitator, or system designer/mediator?[15]

In 2006, mediator Lisa Jo Frech and I co-mediated two hybrid mediation/Creative Problem Solving sessions.[16] The group was in conflict over the contentious prospect of bringing an ecologically sensitive area into the Urban Growth Boundary (UGB) around Portland, Oregon. The UGB is controlled by Metro, a unique regional government entity with jurisdiction over land use planning for the entire Portland metropolitan area.

Our task was two-fold: 1) help a local land conservancy group find creative solutions to reduce polarization by resolving issues among the stakeholders, and 2) test the combined group's willingness and ability to move toward consensus. Six people with very diverse interests requested that the mediation between two

Using Affirmative Judgment

- Look at the advantages of an idea.

Ask, "What's good about it?"

- Consider the potential of an idea.

Ask, "In what ways might it work?"

- Then think about the limitations or concerns you have about the idea.

Ask, "In what ways might I overcome those concerns?"

Stay positive and future focused.

> Scott Isaksen, Brian Dorval, & Donald Treffinger,
> *Creative Approaches to Problem Solving*,
> pp. 48-50.

contentious groups be conducted in a Creative Problem Solving Workshop format.

At the first meeting we introduced ourselves and the hybrid mediation/CPS process. Our brief lecture provided time for the participants to settle in and decide whether they could trust us. I introduced them to my squeaky dog toy approach to crowd control. A wall chart visually demonstrated similarities between mediation and CPS. The agreement to mediate was finally signed after considerable discussion about their initial need for absolute confidentiality. Tension remained high throughout the confidentiality discussion.

The group's working assumption was that the developer among them was their enemy. As soon as the participants introduced themselves, the developer, with a background in planning, for the first time expressed his commitment to protecting the natural environment. New information! Prior to the meeting, nobody had thought to ask him what his interests were. The negativity in the room immediately dropped away.

Next, the group developed, as a Problem Statement, the question, "How can we have development that increases current UGB *while* protecting critical resources including water quality and natural habitat?" We introduced the tool SCAMPER,[17] an idea generating list of questions shown in the *Workbook*. The questions encouraged their Reticular Activating Systems to deliberately focus on a variety of ways of looking at their ideas. Creative solutions were invited. To avoid debate we required that all ideas begin with the phrases *"In what ways might we ...?"* or *"How to ...?"* My squeaky toy was at the ready to maintain order as necessary.

At the beginning of the second meeting the group signed a revised agreement to mediate with the usual space for exceptions to confidentiality. The group agreed to allow the following entities to be informed of their agreement: their non-profit boards and staffs, the area landowners, the Homebuilders Association, county governments, the City of Portland, affected state agencies, the Audubon Society, plus 19 others! The group laughed in recognition that the long, inclusive list rendered moot their earlier distrust and need for confidentiality.

As they continued generating creative solutions, while addressing their diverse concerns, it became readily apparent that

> An artfully crafted position is often the best and most efficient way of defining the conflict or setting the stage for effective problem-solving activities.
>
> Bernard Mayer, *Beyond Neutrality*, p. 126.

they had successfully reached their goal of testing their willingness and ability to move toward collaboration. The trust level was so high that the group did not feel the need to sign a formal agreement document.

Although they loved the hybrid CPS/mediation model, they later ran into an insurmountable block to their continued creative work. One prophetic evaluation comment said it all: "Without funding to continue, the process will come to a grinding halt. The process budget is too small." The participants were not compensated for time to build relationships, only for such concrete things as the miles of trails built and acres protected. A major disadvantage of being out in front of an issue is that non-profit organizations lack the unrestricted funds to take time to create alliances between groups with seemingly incompatible goals. However, through their experience they proved to themselves that future contentious negotiations will be much more successful if stakeholders are given opportunities to know each other as people before sitting across from each other as adversaries.

What hybrid models do you use? Which might you consider utilizing? How might you maintain the integrity of the mediation process while enhancing the parties' creativity? And, as always, what's stopping you?

What grows out of our interactions with others? Through exchange and mutual sharing—and through our differences—we move toward deeper understandings and an expanded point of view, one that would be impossible to reach alone, in our isolated, subjective ponderings. Together, we attract energy and discover creative solutions in a manner we cannot accomplish by ourselves.

> David Ulrich,
> *The Widening Stream: The Seven Stages of Creativity*, p. 240.

CHAPTER ELEVEN

The Authors' Dialogue Creatively Continues

Now that you have expanded your vision of yourself as a creative mediator I invite you to apply your creative thinking and strategies to the necessary task of transforming the future of the fields of conflict engagement and mediation.

Authors Mayer,[1] Lederach,[2] and Lang and Taylor,[3] have all concluded their books with extensive comments about what they believe needs to happen to transform the field. As my contribution to the ongoing dialogue, I have taken the liberty of reframing some of these authors' challenges and questions into open-ended language to encourage and facilitate your creative thinking. For example:

> "Mediators should be flexible in developing and testing their formulations; they should remain open to new information ... mediators who enact a reflective approach must not only experiment; they must also suspend judgment and question assumptions."[4]

Unfortunately the statement is filled with "shoulds" and "musts" which causes neurological dead ends; barriers to creative responses. When questions and statements are reframed as positive and future focused your Reticular Activating System is more readily able to connect to possible solutions. Listen to how much different the above phrases sound when broken into components, then reframed using the positive and thought-provoking questions beginning with *"In what ways might we ...?"* and *"How might we ...?"*

"Mediators should be flexible in developing and testing their formulations" becomes *"In what ways might we* be flexible in developing and testing formulations?" Next, "They should remain open to new information" becomes *"How might we* remain open to new information?" Finally, the statement "Mediators who

We know so much about the problems of the world today that it's easy to fall into fear and denial. What we need is a language of hope and possibility that's grounded in ideas and experiences emerging from innovators in science, business, and communities.

> Peter Senge, et al.,
> *Presence: An Exploration of Profound Change in People, Organizations, and Society*, p. 218.

enact a reflective approach must not only experiment; they must also suspend judgment and question assumptions" is divided into two questions: "*In what ways might we* enact a reflective approach?" and "*How might we* suspend our judgment and question our assumptions?" Did responses to these questions already come to your mind?

In 2004, Mayer[5] noted that although mediation has been offered for the past forty years, the services are not yet being more fully utilized. Mayer concluded that the reason is related to both our dependence on the role of neutral, and to our basic definition of ourselves as conflict resolvers. Mayer recommends that we broaden our definition of ourselves as mediators to include recognition of our knowledge of conflict and the variety of ways conflict can be approached. Mayer maintains that we need to see and promote ourselves as "conflict specialists" who have particular knowledge of the dynamics of conflict, conceptual tools to assist people develop constructive approaches to conflict, and intervention strategies that can be used to assist people involved in conflict.

How do we do that? Once we have rebranded ourselves as Mayer suggests, what else is needed to creatively expand our intervention services? One answer can be found in creativity research[6] that identifies seven major social elements necessary to ensure success in any given field. They are: training, monitoring, resources, hope, opportunity, reward, and recognition. When these elements are reframed as social elements necessary for success in the field of mediation, they offer intriguing insights.

A Blinding Flash of the Obvious is that these elements are in short supply in the field of conflict resolution. The first two, basic mediation training and initial monitoring, are required to fulfill minimum training requirements. But the next requirement, financial resources to increase individual mediator development, is not always readily available. This, in turn, reduces possibilities for the rest of the elements: hope, opportunities, rewards and recognition.

One way to transform the mediation field is to apply aspects of the creative process to the challenge of rebranding and promoting ourselves as "conflict specialists." To this end, I reframed more questions asked by Lang and Taylor, Mayer, and Lederach into Creative Problem Solving statements. I then categorized

Social Conditions Necessary for Creative Achievement

Training
Monitoring
Resources
Hope
Opportunity
Reward
Recognition

> Mihaly Csikszentmihalyi,
> *Creativity: Flow and the Psychology of Discovery and Invention*, pp. 330-335.

them according to the seven social conditions needed for creative achievement. The resulting seven questions, listed below, and more extensively in my *Workbook*, are all broad, brief, beneficial, and free of limiting criteria. This format offers the maximum opportunity for divergent, right-brained, expansive thinking. Put your Reticular Activating System to work as you read and mentally respond to them. As Judy Teufel, my old pottery friend is fond of saying, "No guts, no glory."

Training / Professional Development

In what ways might learning, creativity, and professional development be encouraged beyond just the attainment of a particular set of standards?

Monitoring / Standards of Practice

How might we incorporate concerns about confidentiality?... concerns about ethical dilemmas?... issues of qualifications?

Resources / Marketing

How might we creatively adapt to the changing financial conditions we are facing?... social conditions we are facing?

Hope / Making of Careers

In what ways might professional organizations in our field take an increased role in stimulating professional development?

Opportunity

How might we create more opportunities for conflict resolvers to be advocates in some cases while neutral in others?

Reward

How might necessary resources be generated to increase mediators' professional development?

Recognition

How might mediators be visibly acknowledged for their essentially invisible work?

> Effective marketing will come from a clear self-concept, from being creative in adapting to new opportunities, from continually refining our offerings, and from being willing to present new services and approaches assertively and with confidence.
>
> Bernard Mayer, *Beyond Neutrality*, p. 287.

Did you think of some ideas? To generate even more, it is time for a SCAMPER-like mix-and-match:

- What words might be **Substituted** to provide for clarity or appropriateness?
- Which of these questions might be **Combined** with others?
- In what ways might they be **Adapted** to your program or practice?
- How might they be **Modified**, or **Maximized**, or **Minimized**?
- How might these ideas presented be **Put to Additional Uses**?
- What questions need to be **Eliminated**?
- What might be **Reversed** or put in a more appropriate order in which to consider them?

Did these additional questions further jar your thinking? In what ways might we continue the conversation? More ideas are found on my website: www.MediatingwithPicasso.com. Please add yours. The challenge needs your creative thinking.

Some of these questions are being answered in innovative programs and initiatives that already exist nationwide. The following are four I am familiar with in the Portland, Oregon metropolitan area. I offer them as examples of how the field is expanding, because it is easier to adapt an existing innovation than to generate a new one. Consider ways in which they might be adapted to your locale.

The first example involves the police. Since 2004, Portland Police Bureau officers, along with police departments in New York City, Washington D.C. and Denver, have participated in police/citizen mediations. Officers attend while on duty, armed and in uniform. There is no expectation of a signed agreement. Issues generally involve police courtesy and conduct.

City residents request mediation for a variety of reasons. In one situation, police responded to a call about youths creating a disturbance at a transit stop. An innocent bystander was swept up in the action and wrongly issued a citation. In another case, a man driving past a rally honked in support of gay marriage. He felt he was stopped and cited by an officer who did not agree with

> Upgrading one's imagination about what is possible is always a leap of faith ... Throwing off old constraints won't lead us to a world of no constraints. All worlds, past, present and future, have constraints; throwing off the old ones just creates a space for new ones to emerge.
>
> > Clay Shirky,
> > *Cognitive Surplus: Creativity and Generosity in a Connected Age*, p. 162.

his political views. A Latino man believed he was falsely charged and racially profiled when his car was towed after a traffic stop. A woman complained that officers, responding to a dispute between her and her neighbor, unfairly sided with the neighbor and were rude. An African-American homeowner complained of racial profiling after he was arrested by a "rookie cop" for "taking out the garbage while black."

Police/citizen mediations are often transformative. You already read about the officer and attorney who talked for over an hour as I sat quietly by. They both needed to tell their story, even though the resident refused to sign the agreement to mediate. I have witnessed apologies offered and accepted on both sides as each party gained a greater understanding of the other's perspective. In my experience, police/citizen cases embody the intent of community policing, one community member and one officer at a time.

In what ways might the police/citizen mediation programs be duplicated in every city and town in America? What creative blocks prevent you from considering the possibility?

My second example involves juveniles. In 2006 mediator Grace Reed began using her personal story to reach 13-to-17 year old addicted boys, who were part of Multnomah County's restorative justice Residential Alcohol/Drug (RAD) Project. Because she also has a degree in drama therapy, Grace was accepted as a drama teacher for the Chances for Choices Project: conflict resolution within the restorative justice/transformation mediation movement.[7] The project was part of Grace's research in creative expression for her Portland State University conflict resolution master's degree.

On her first visit there, after passing three security check points, she entered the classroom and sat quietly until the boys' curiosity overcame the chaos they were causing. Their assumption was that she was just another do-good "grandma cookie lady." Then she asked, "Where do you want your X?" Meaning, when did they want to die? She then told them her own personal story of survival from youthful addiction, abuse, and abandonment.[8]

> On June 3rd, 1980, she was sitting at her living room table in Van Nuys, California, with a bottle of Wild Turkey, a line of cocaine, a loaded clip, the German Luger laying to her right. She sat half the night drinking, shot glass by shot

> ... on an average day 7,500 youth are in adult jails ... A federal law to keep youth out of adult prison has been on the books for over three decades. Come on society, we can do better than this!... Do we dare believe, we as a nation have the right to ignore and misunderstand this mess? We need restorative justice models that are designed to transform lives now more than ever before.
>
> Grace E. Reed, *Needs*, p. 76.

glass, the amber whiskey sliding smoothly down her core, warming her cold heart, a ritual she had done for years. When she was done, she snorted the line, slapped the clip into the Luger, put the barrel to her right temple and pulled the trigger.

Her story gained their immediate attention and their trust. Through creative writing exercises Grace began giving them more chances for better choices. As one of their first projects they wrote a play, "The Children of the Other Shoe." The ten-page script "stays true to the essence of what at-risk youth are trying to say to themselves, each other and the outside world where the reality and impact of our compromised systems, including the justice system, and our concerned communities live and act."[9] In 2007, Grace arranged for the boys to watch their play performed by the Portland State University theater department.

The skills the boys learned in the after-release component of the residential alcohol/drug program helped them navigate peer pressure once they were back out in the community. They provided strategies for the boys to continue to use their innate, still intact, obvious creativity and provided balance toward making better and healthy choices. The skills they learned were designed to help them reduce addiction problems, and boost their choice-oriented thinking to achieve long term sobriety and freedom from crime.

However, intense peer pressure on the street causes recidivism to occur. The odds of the boys staying clean and sober are low. The boys are often forced to make bad choices that put them back into the juvenile justice system. Yet, from time to time, Grace sees one of "her" boys on the street. They are living proof that her drama therapy and its tools can positively effect this population, in terms of their self-concept, social interaction, critical thinking, and decision making.

How might this kind of Chances for Choices Project be expanded to give more struggling, conflicted youth the skills they need? How might it give them more positive choices upon their release so they can stay clean, sober, and free from crime?

The third example is from the City of Beaverton, a suburb of Portland, which has a mediation program that provides residents additional conflict specialist roles that do not necessarily involve mediation. A broader perspective on their role as "conflict spe-

... there are many other ways in which we can assist people in conflict without acting as neutral third parties. If we view ourselves as conflict specialists ... a whole new range of opportunities opens up for how we can deal with conflict constructively and dramatically. We can then be in a better position to help people engage instead of avoid, listen instead of attack, organize instead of retreat, connect instead of isolate, and much more. In this way, we can help transform the way conflict is conducted.

> Bernard Mayer,
> *Beyond Neutrality*, pp. 117-118.

cialists" has shaped the way they have defined their program. In the future it may be more appropriate for them to call themselves a Conflict Consulting Center.[10]

The Beaverton program has organically incorporated creative problem solving approaches as they have expanded their program to include the roles of conflict coach, advisor, strategist, facilitator, and educator. As conflict coaches, Beaverton volunteers now do more pre-mediation preparation, resulting in disputants coming to the table better prepared to negotiate. They also help parties minimize their differences with the city before attending planning commission meetings.

In one situation, a woman called for support regarding letters that she had received from her home owners association (HOA) board. Within an hour a volunteer mediator had helped her identify issues, discuss the history of the dispute, and develop a proposal, including a request for mediation for her to take to the board.

In another situation, Beaverton homeowners discovered that their HOA board was secretly planning a major fee assessment of HOA members. The conflict quickly became personal. The board and residents agreed to a facilitated meeting to identify specific issues. Mediator volunteers helped the residents develop a list of specific questions and concerns, and helped them consider options for moving forward. The board and residents communicated their concerns and needs more effectively, and worked together to resolve their differences. One resident said that this was the first time that the community had actually come together instead of acting separately as individuals.

In another case, neighbors who had already made their own agreement about a fence construction and boundary issue called Jim Brooks, Beaverton's program manager, to report that they needed him to come right away to resolve an urgent issue. The contractor had installed the fence posts and the concrete was drying. Jim immediately drove to their homes. When he arrived one party said, "We want you to tell us the best solution." As he read their agreement, Jim could see how it might be misinterpreted. So, while the contractor waited, the neighbors discussed options and arrived at a decision that both parties were happy with.

"You're not going to make us sit in the same room together are you?" asked the attorney who called to set up a mediation

To maintain a sustained commitment, we need a larger vision, a broader purpose, and ideas—our own guiding light. When we have an abiding aim, one that can be counted on to offer both challenge and nourishment, we are already well on the way ... Ego cannot sustain the kind of energy and commitment that we need for our most significant work and contributions. What does it take to give something our best energies and efforts, often for years, without external rewards of public recognition?

> David Ulrich,
> *The Widening Stream: The Seven Stages of Creativity*, p. 129.

session. In response, the Beaverton program has become more flexible in the variety of mediation models they offer participants. They collaboratively worked out a process that accommodates the program's desire to have the parties discuss their issues directly while preserving the attorney's need to caucus separately with his clients to develop proposals to bring to the table. As a result, they now have more attorneys attending mediation sessions.

Jim Brooks, Beaverton's director, puts it this way. "Remember, each time we are involved in a conflict we have an opportunity to make a choice about what kind of community we want."[11]

In what ways might you expand your view of what community mediators can do? What mediation cultural barriers prevent you from considering them? How might you overcome those barriers?

Community Mediators

Finally, the City of Portland has developed a unique community dialogue program to facilitate difficult conversations. This innovative restorative justice program addresses racial tensions surrounding the gentrification of previously all-black neighborhoods.[12] Meetings are sponsored by the City of Portland's Office of Neighborhood Involvement (ONI). Judith Mowry, Effective Engagement Solutions Program Specialist, invites new, mostly white, residents of gentrified housing to attend monthly meetings with their long-standing, mostly black, neighbors.

The meetings are held at local black churches. African American community leaders are invited to speak to their new neighbors. They describe the harm gentrification has caused to the cohesiveness of their neighborhoods. The new residents' gain a greater understanding of the harm from the perspective of those who are harmed, which builds a foundation for further steps in the healing process.

The results of the meetings have been profound. New and old residents return, month after month, meeting in small discussion groups to respond to the speakers' comments. They have come to realize that the impact of the harm is not related to the intent of the new-comers. The meetings promote reconciliation, building and rebuilding relationships and mutual responsibility for constructive responses to wrongdoing with the community.

These projects are examples of the many other ways mediators can expand their services to become conflict specialists. How might your community initiate such projects and dialogues? In what ways might your diverse community members be involved in the planning? Once again, what's stopping you?

We shall not cease from exploration
And the end of all our exploring
Will be to arrive where we started
And know the place for the first time.

T.S. Elliot, *Little Gidding V.*

CHAPTER TWELVE

Conclusion

This book is my contribution to the ongoing dialogue within the mediation community. It is my response to authors' views that mediators need to be more creative. I have presented a myriad of reasons why you already are creative and demonstrated ways you can increase your creativity as you mediate.

By reading *Picasso* you have had the chance to experience for yourself my BFOs regarding creative architects and their correlations to creative mediators, and between Creative Problem Solving and mediation processes. Perhaps my greatest BFO is that mediation's real magic is our own positivity and our ability to increase the positivity of people in disputes.

By reading *Picasso* you have opened your Johari Window, releasing unconscious barriers to your creative thinking. You have gained a new understanding of the historical attitudes and assumptions that made creative people vulnerable to ridicule. You have gained a sense of your creative style, your type, and your most and least important values. Your deliberate impartiality is increased as a result. You have heard my *Tales from the Hospital Crypt* about a specific Red Queen and examined personas you inhabit when dealing with RQs and other difficult people. You attended my virtual Myers-Briggs and Naked Truth workshops, experiencing both concepts at the ground level. You have completed thirteen self-assessments in the *Workbook* and completed your Individual Creativity Profile.

Conflicts of every kind call for more self-aware, creative and compassionate people who are willing and able to be part of the solution. Einstein called for new modes of thinking; creative thinking. I am convinced that now that you have a greater understanding of creativity and a greater belief in your own, you can respond more creatively to challenges facing the nation and the

... positivity is renewable ... each of us can choose to seed more of it into our lives. As these seeds grow we flourish. We become full of possibility, remarkably resilient and happy. We contribute. With more positivity, we can create both the life we want and a world worth leaving to our children.

Barbara Fredrickson, *Positivity*, p. 36.

world, let alone the field of mediation.

As Mayer has stated, the greatest challenge to the field of alternative dispute resolution and peacemaking is to find ways to reframe our vision; to think of ourselves and the work we do in a different way. We need to be able to project our role more broadly and creatively.[1] To do that, we need to move beyond whatever assumptions, fears, and blocks hold us back from doing so. My hope is that you are now convinced you are more creative than you thought you were when you started reading *Picasso*. Even those of you who did not think you needed convincing.

Go ahead, declare your creativity! No guts, no glory! "There is nothing enlightened about shrinking so that other people won't feel insecure around you ... as you let your own light shine, you unconsciously give other people permission to do the same. As you are liberated from your own fear, your presence automatically liberates others."[2] Once you acknowledge your own unique strengths, you can apply your experienced optimism, positivity and creativity to the challenges currently facing the field of mediation; challenges that are calling for creative responses.

My invitation to you is for you to consider what you now know about yourself as a creative person and apply it to those challenges. In what ways can you further the professional dialogue? In what ways might you join in the discussion and contribute more productive ideas for the professional development of mediation? Again, what's stopping you?

Your inherent whole brain complex creative thinking better prepares you to meet "new challenges with flexibility, inventiveness, and imagination, and with the ability to grasp complex arrays of inter-connected ideas and facts, to perceive underlying patterns of events, and to see old problems in new ways."[3] I believe that this is how we, as mediators and peacemakers, are responding to Albert Einstein's disturbing caution.

We are responding because we can. By using our positivity to help disputants make new creative connections between their right and left hemispheres, we literally help them create new ways of thinking. In the process we transform the parties for the better, whatever their definition of that may be.

I remain as convinced as I was when I had my first intuitive Blinding Flash of the Obvious 25 years ago. We, as experienced, dedicated mediators, exhibit creative and self-actualizing traits in

We can't be creative if we refuse to be confused. Change always starts with confusion; cherished interpretations must dissolve to make way for the new. Of course it's scary to give up what we know, but the abyss is where newness lives. Great ideas and inventions miraculously appear in the space of not knowing. If we can move through the fear and enter the abyss, we are rewarded greatly. We rediscover we're creative.

>Margaret Wheatley,
>*Turning to One Another*, p. 37.

our socialization and interpersonal behavior. It shows up in the richness and complexity of our psychological development, and our degree of mental health. I maintain that without these traits we could not be effective mediators.

I believe that as mediators we are alchemists, able to transmute poison. If not always turning it into gold, at least transmuting it into a benign substance safe to be near.

I believe that our alchemy lies in our ability to invoke positivity within the parties. We bring peace into the room simply by increasing the ratio of positivity to negativity in what the parties are experiencing.

I believe that as mediators we have the obligation to be optimistic. Not a saccharine optimism devoid of real-world experience, but an experienced optimism from the dozens, if not hundreds of times we have been privileged to witness people applying their own creativity to seemingly hopeless disputes.

I believe our purpose as mediators is to find that kernel of possibility that lies within the most intractable conflicts. That purpose, like Garrison Keillor's Lake Wobegon Powdermilk Biscuits, gives us the strength to do what needs to be done.

I believe that this can best happen through a shift in our identity toward being more creative mediators who "think like Picasso."

I firmly believe creativity is relevant in conflict situations. Now, more than ever, all forms of conflict resolution are needed. As mediators we have the creative ability to expand our thinking. We can become the architects of new forms of dispute resolution, on the local, regional, national, and even global level. We only have to believe that we can.

ACKNOWLEDGMENTS

Special thanks to Robert Mandelson for his honest critiques of the early drafts of *Picasso;* Yvonne Coleman for her initial and essential edits; Cynthia Kostka, for her early and necessary coaching; Alexandra Smith, for her ongoing support; Zorwyn Madrone, for her help on the Red Queens chapter; Fran Rosica, for his validation that I was headed in the right direction; Linda Scher, for her Adaptive perspective; Elizabeth Livingston, for her *Alice* expertise; Carolyn McCall and Ailona Dundore for input and recommendations on the MBTI materials; Sam Imperati, for just the jolt I needed; Mary Kay Szynskie, for keeping my brain intact throughout the process; Barbara Blackstone, for her expansive view of the book's possibilities; Grace Reed, for demonstrating how to get it done; Roger Firestien, my graduate advisor, friend and designated kwazy wabbit; Molly Keating, for introducing me to Guadalupe; and to Guadalupe Guajardo, for advising me to put more of me back into *Picasso.*

I also want to acknowledge my many friends, colleagues and Marylhurst University students for their early and constant support and critiques that provided me with the ongoing nudges I needed. Special mention goes to Jeff Sweeney, friend and Communication Department Chair; Cathy Bennett and Katherine Stansbury, former students, supporters and friends. Thanks for the encouragement!

Special thanks and love to my daughters Heidi, Sarah, and Julie, for going along with my Excellent Adventure to Buffalo that started it all. Through the years they have consistently modeled what inherent creativity really looks like. Finally, thanks and love to my husband, David Gleason, for his blessings, support and encouragement.

Glossary

Adaptive creativity: A style preference for improving existing ideas.

Affirmative judgment: A three-stage method of responding to an idea: First, state what is good about it; next, state what potential it has; and last, state concerns about it.

Alpha brain waves: The brain's state of relaxed alertness, bringing a feeling of relaxation and well-being. Inspiration, creativity, heightened memory, increased concentration, and ability to quickly assimilate facts are derived from alpha wave activity.

Army Values: Loyalty, duty, respect, selfless service, honor, integrity, personal courage.

Belief systems: Unconscious, engrained beliefs.

Beta brain waves: The brain's "awake" wavelength when it is transmitting and receiving information.

Bisociating: Holding two, mutually exclusive thoughts at the same time.

Catchment words: Based on common words, catchments are mental funneling systems that constrict a wide variety of inputs to the same output.

Conduit metaphor: An unconscious expression of communication in concrete terms, as if it were a pipeline, and the communication content were obvious to all parties.

Convergent guidelines: CPS rules for deliberate decision making.

Creative Problem Solving (CPS): A comprehensive cognitive and affective system built on one's natural creative processes that deliberately ignites creative thinking and generates creative solutions and change. Incorporates divergent and convergent thinking skills.

Determined creativity: Aristotle's rationalist view that the creative process obeyed natural laws, that it was not possible for anything to be produced if nothing had previously existed.

Divergent guidelines: CPS rules for idea generation.

Flat-brained: Metaphor for the inability to mentally function because of over-stimulation or stress.

Flow: Remaining in a highly focused state of consciousness while facing a clear set of goals that require immediate and appropriate responses. Deeply involved in a self-contained universe, unaware of time or effort; apart from ordinary life.

Hard-wired metaphors: Widespread conceptual metaphors formed when common sensory and physical/motor (sensorimotor) experiences become linked in the brain with feelings and ideas.

Innovative creativity: A style preference for challenging the current paradigms.

Johari Window: A model for describing the process of human interaction, from very limited to very open.

KAI: Kirton Adaption-Innovation Inventory.

Kepner-Tregoe Model: A problem solving model that seeks one correct answer to a problem.

Kirton Adaption-Innovation Inventory: Measures styles of creativity on a continuum from Adaptive to Innovative.

Mental frames: Hardwired metaphors and associative experiences that form a framework or lens in which one sees the world.

Middles: A measure of those whose creative style is between Adaptive and Innovative.

MBTI: Myers-Briggs Type Indicator.

Myers-Briggs Type Indicator: Describes how people take in information, how they make decisions based on that information, and their corresponding reactions, values, motivations, skills and interests.

Nurturing Parent metaphor: Assumes that the world is good and can be made a better place. Morality begins with empathy, the ability to understand others and feel what they feel. Assumes responsibility for oneself, for protection and care of those who need care, and for larger community.

Personas: Conscious extensions of real or fictional roles played in real life.

Primary metaphors: Hard-wired metaphors needed to conceptualize abstract thought.

Psychological androgyny: Having the psychological characteristics of both women and men.

Radical creation: An idea or concept not easily traced to preceding ideas or concepts; undetermined creativity.

RAS: Reticular Activating System.

Red Queens: Metaphor for those exhibiting characteristics of narcissistic personality disorder.

RQ: Red Queen.

Reticular activating system: That part of the brain that pays attention to some things while ignoring others. Turns on thoughts, emotions or both.

SCAMPER: An acronym to help someone remember to substitute, combine, adapt, modify, put to other uses, eliminate, and reverse ideas when brainstorming.

Scotomas: Mental blind spots. Inability to comprehend information that conflicts with existing paradigm or belief system.

Self-actualizing creativity: Acknowledging the potential for creativity and self-actualization in everyone. Self-actualizing creative people are mentally healthy, live fully productive lives, approach all aspects of their lives in a flexible, creative fashion. Not necessarily brilliantly creative in a specialized area. They want to realize their potential, to become everything they are capable of becoming. Includes an ever-increasing move toward unity and integration, a synergy within the person.

Situational Leadership in mediation: The type of leadership deployed during a mediation. Depends on the needs, actions and behaviors of the parties.

Special Talent creativity: High level creativity in a specific area: music, sports, science.

Strict Father metaphor: Assumes that the world is clear-cut and absolute. Correlates morality with prosperity through self-interest. Belief that entire model must be perpetuated, leaving little room for negotiation or compromise.

Styles of creativity: Orientation to problem solving; either an adaptive style, a preference for improving existing ideas, or an innovative style, a preference for challenging the current paradigms

Synectics: A model of problem solving that emphasizes making the familiar strange and the strange familiar.

Undetermined creativity: Plato's explanation of the source of creativity. Independent of natural and human resources. The work of their divine source of inspiration, the Muse.

Chapter Notes

MY OPENING STATEMENT

1. H. Gardner, *Creating Minds: An Anatomy of Creativity as Seen through the Lives of Freud, Einstein, Picasso, Stravinsky, Eliot, Graham, and Gandhi* (New York: Basic Books, 1993), 145.
2. J.P. Lederach, *The Moral Imagination: The Art and Soul of Building Peace* (New York: Oxford University Press, 2005), 173.
3. J. Schell, "The Fate of the Earth," New York: Alfred A. Knopf, 1982, 188, quoted in L. Neilson, *Impact of Creative Problem Solving Training: An In Depth Evaluation of a Six Day Course in Creative Problem Solving* (Unpublished master's project. SUNY College of Buffalo, Buffalo, NY 1990), 2.
4. J. Driscoll, "Defense Workers Shift Gears: Confronting Ethical Dilemmas in the Workplace," *Plowshare Press* Autumn, 1988, quoted in L. Neilson, *Impact of Creative Problem Solving Training: An In Depth Evaluation of a Six Day Course in Creative Problem Solving* (Unpublished master's project. SUNY College of Buffalo, Buffalo, NY 1990), 3.
5. B.S. Mayer, *Beyond Neutrality: Confronting the Crisis in Conflict Resolution* (San Francisco: Jossey-Bass, 2004), 295.

CHAPTER ONE – BACKGROUND INFORMATION

1. W. Ury and R. Fisher, *Getting Past No: Negotiating with Difficult People* (New York: Bantam Books, 1999).
2. Mayer, *Beyond Neutrality: Confronting the Crisis in Conflict Resolution*, 117.
3. Ibid., 146-147.
4. M.D. Lang and A. Taylor, *The Making of a Mediator: Developing Artistry in Practice* (San Francisco: Jossey-Bass, 2000),

232.

5. M. Csikszentmihalyi, *Finding Flow: The Psychology of Engagement in Everyday Life* (New York: HarperCollins, 1997).

6. A. Koestler, *Insight and Outlook: An Inquiry into Common Foundations of Science, Art and Social Ethics* (Lincoln, NB: University of Nebraska Press, 1949), 36-38.

7. J.W. Reitman, "The Personal Qualities of the Mediator: Taking Time for Reflection and Renewal," in *Bringing Peace into the Room*, eds. D. Bowling and D. Hoffman (San Francisco: Jossey-Bass, 2003), 241-242.

8. E. de Bono, *de Bono's Thinking Course* (revised) (New York: Facts on File, Inc., 1994), 53-70.

9. P. Adler, "Unintentional Excellence: An Exploration of Mastery and Incompetence," in *Bringing Peace into the Room*, eds. D. Bowling and D. Hoffman (San Francisco: Jossey-Bass, 2003), 57-75.

10. R.D. Benjamin, "Managing the Natural Energy of Conflict: Mediators, Tricksters, and the Constructive Use of Deception," in *Bringing Peace into the Room*, eds. D. Bowling and D. Hoffman (San Francisco: Jossey-Bass, 2003), 79-134.

11. M. LeBaron, "Trickster, Mediator's Friend," in *Bringing Peace into the Room*, eds. D. Bowling and D. Hoffman (San Francisco: Jossey-Bass, 2003), 135-150.

12. Lederach, *The Moral Imagination: The Art and Soul of Building Peace*, 38.

13. Lang and Taylor, *The Making of a Mediator: Developing Artistry in Practice*, 232.

14. J. Jaynes, *The Origins of Consciousness in the Breakdown of the Bicameral Mind* (Boston: Houghton Mifflin, 1976), 17.

15. J.J. Ratey, *A User's Guide to the Brain: Perception, Attention, and the Four Theaters of the Brain* (New York: Vintage Books, 2002), 114.

16. Jaynes, *The Origins of Consciousness in the Breakdown of the Bicameral Mind*, 17.

17. G. Dryden and J. Vos, *The Learning Revolution: A Lifelong Learning Programme for the World's Finest Computer: Your*

Amazing Brain! (Torrance, CA: Jalmar Press, 1994), 118-121.
18. J.L. Adams, *Conceptual Blockbusting: A Guide to Better Ideas*, 3rd ed. (Reading, MA: Addison-Wesley Publishing Co., 1986), 29-31.

CHAPTER TWO – A BLINDING FLASH OF THE OBVIOUS

1. D.W. MacKinnon, "Architects, Personality Types, and Creativity" (1965), in *The Creativity Question*, eds. A. Rothenberg and C.R. Hausman (Durham, NC: Duke University Press, 1976), 176.
2. Ibid.
3. A.H. Maslow, *The Farther Reaches of Human Nature* (New York: Viking Press, 1971), Table I, 308-9.
4. Ibid.
5. A.H. Maslow, *Toward a Psychology of Being*, 2nd ed. (Princeton, NJ: Van Nostrand, 1968), 138.
6. ibid., 137.
7. M.E.P. Seligman and M. Csikszentmihalyi, "Positive Psychology: An Introduction," *American Psychologist* 55, no. 1 (2000): 5-14, cited in B.L. Fredrickson, *Positivity* (New York: Crown Publishers, 2009), 181.
8. B.L. Fredrickson, *Positivity* (New York: Random House, 2009), 6.
9. Ibid., 57-58.
10. Ibid., 16.
11. Ibid., 9.
12. Dryden and Vos, *The Learning Revolution: A Lifelong Learning Programme for the World's Finest Computer: Your Amazing Brain!* 118-121.
13. Organisation for Economic Co-operation and Development, *Understanding the Brain: The Birth of a Learning Science* (Paris, France: Centre for Educational Research and Innovation, 2007).
14. E.P. Torrance, *The Search for Satori and Creativity* (Buffalo, NY: Creative Education Foundation, 1979), 12.
15. J.P. Guilford, "Creativity Research: Past, Present, Future,"

in *Frontiers of Creativity Research: Beyond the Basics*, ed. S. G. Isaksen (Buffalo, NY: Bearly Limited, 1987), 33-65.

16. A. Koestler, *The Act of Creation* (New York: Dell Publishing Company, 1964), 35.
17. Dryden and Vos, *The Learning Revolution: A Lifelong Learning Programme for the World's Finest Computer: Your Amazing Brain!* 127-129.
18. Dryden and Vos, *The Learning Revolution: A Lifelong Learning Programme for the World's Finest Computer: Your Amazing Brain!* 127-129.
19. M. Csikszentmihalyi, *Creativity: Flow and the Psychology of Discovery and Invention* (New York: HarperCollins, 1996), 27-75.
20. Maslow, *Toward a Psychology of Being*, 139.
21. Fredrickson, *Positivity*, 62-63.
22. Maslow, *Toward a Psychology of Being*, 138.
23. D. Ackerman, *The Alchemy of the Brain: The Marvel and Mystery of the Brain* (New York: Scribner, 2004), 93.
24. Csikszentmihalyi, *Creativity: Flow and the Psychology of Discovery and Invention*, 58-76.
25. D. Bowling and D. Hoffman, eds., *Bringing Peace into the Room* (San Francisco: Jossey-Bass, 2003), 92.
26. Csikszentmihalyi, *Creativity: Flow and the Psychology of Discovery and Invention*, 57-75.

CHAPTER THREE – BARRIERS TO CREATIVE THINKING

1. G. Lakoff and M. Johnson, *Philosophy in the Flesh: The Embodied Mind and its Challenge to Western Thought* (New York: Basic Books, 1999), 45.
2. L. Pitts, "Ignore the Facts, If Your Mind Is Made Up," *The Miami Herald,* April 16, 2007.
3. Lakoff and Johnson, *Philosophy in the Flesh: The Embodied Mind and its Challenge to Western Thought*, 77.
4. Fredrickson, *Positivity*, 55.
5. Ibid., 127.
6. Ibid., 33.

7. J.M. Gottman, *What Predicts Divorce? The Relationship between Marital Processes and Marital Outcomes* (Hillsdale, NJ: Lawrence Erlbaum Associates, 1994), cited in B.L. Fredrickson, *Positivity* (New York: Crown Publishers, 2009), 136.
8. Ibid., 138.
9. J. Luft, *Of Human Interaction* (Palo Alto, CA: National Press, 1969), 177.
10. J. Luft, *Group Processes: An Introduction to Group Dynamics*, 5th ed. (Palto Alto, CA: National Press Books, 1970).

CHAPTER FOUR – HISTORICAL ATTITUDES TOWARD CREATIVITY

1. S.G. Isaksen, ed., *Frontiers of Creativity Research: Beyond the Basics* (Buffalo, NY: Bearly Limited, 1987), 1-3.
2. Jaynes, *The Origins of Consciousness in the Breakdown of the Bicameral Mind*, 69.
3. A. Rothenberg and C.R. Hausman, eds., *The Creativity Question* (Durham, NC: Duke University Press, 1976), 31-37.
4. F. Galton, "Hereditary Genius: An Inquiry into Its Laws and Consequences" (1869), in *The Creativity Question*, eds. A. Rothenberg and C.R. Hausman (Durham, NC: Duke University Press, 1976), 42-48.
5. C. Lombroso, "Genius and Insanity" (1895), in *The Creativity Question*, eds. A. Rothenberg and C.R. Hausman (Durham, NC: Duke University Press, 1976), 79-86.
6. N.C. Andreasen, *The Creating Brain: The Neuroscience of Genius* (New York: Dana Press, 2005), 98.
7. Lombroso, "Genius and Insanity," 79-82.
8. O. Rank, "Life and Creation" (1932), in *The Creativity Question*, eds. A. Rothenberg and C.R. Hausman (Durham, NC: Duke University Press, 1976), 114-120.
9. E. Kris, "On Preconscious Mental Processes" (1952), in *The Creativity Question*, eds. A. Rothenberg and C.R. Hausman (Durham, NC: Duke University Press, 1976), 135-143.
10. L. S. Kubie, "Creation and Neurosis" (1958), in *The Creativity Question*, eds. A. Rothenberg and C.R. Hausman (Durham, NC: Duke University Press, 1976), 143-148.

11. E. Rogers, *Diffusion of Innovations*, 4th ed. (New York: Simon and Schuster, 1995).
12. Guilford, "Creativity Research: Past, Present, Future," 33-45.
13. S. Parnes, "The Creative Studies Project" (1973), in *Frontiers of Creativity Research: Beyond the Basics*, ed. S.G. Isaksen (Buffalo, NY: Bearly Limited, 1987), 156-188.
14. R.L. Firestien, *Leading on the Creative Edge: Gaining Competitive Advantage Through the Power of Creative Problem Solving* (Colorado Springs, CO: Pinon Press, 1996), 21.
15. Parnes, "The Creative Studies Project," 156-188.

CHAPTER FIVE – WHAT'S YOUR STYLE?
1. M.J. Kirton, ed., *Adaptors and Innovators: Styles of Creativity and Problem Solving* (London: Routledge, 1994), 8-11.
2. Ibid.
3. M.J. Kirton, "Adaptors and Innovators: A Description and Measure," *Journal of Applied Psychology* 61, no. 5 (1976): 622-629.
4. Ibid.
5. M.J. Kirton, *Adaption-Innovation: In the Context of Diversity and Change* (London: Routledge, 2003), 106-107.
6. Ibid., 247-254.

CHAPTER SIX – WHAT'S YOUR TYPE?
1. I.B. Myers, M.H. McCaulley, N.L. Quenk, and A.L. Hammer, *Manual: A Guide to the Development and Use of the Myers-Briggs Type Indicator*, 3rd ed. (Palo Alto, CA: Consulting Psychologists Press, 1998), 21-33.
2. Ibid.
3. J. Block and A.M. Kremen, "IQ and Ego-Resiliency: Conceptual and Empirical Connections and Separateness," *Journal of Personality and Social Psychology* 70, no. 2 (1996): 349-361, quoted in B.L. Fredrickson, *Positivity* (New York: Crown Publishers, 2009), 101.
4. Fredrickson, *Positivity*, 106-107.
5. Ibid., 91.
6. G.C. Carne and M.J. Kirton, "Styles of Creativity: Test-Score

Correlations between the Kirton Adaption-Innovation Inventory and the Myers-Briggs Type Indicator.," *Psychological Reports* 50 (1982): 31-36.

7. A. McBroom and C. Goldman, "The Sticky Middle Part: Between the Opening Statement and Agreements," Bellevue, Washington Neighborhood Mediation Program *Update*, January, 2000.

ADDITIONAL BOOKS ABOUT THE MYERS-BRIGGS TYPE INDICATOR
I.B. Myers, *Gifts Differing* (Palo Alto, CA: Consulting Psychologists Press, 1986).
M.E. Loomis, *Dancing the Wheel of Psychological Types* (Wilmette, IL: Chiron, 1991).
M.R. Weisbord, *Discovering Common Ground* (San Francisco: Berret-Koehler, 1992).

CHAPTER SEVEN – WORLD VIEWS AND VALUES

1. Lakoff and Johnson, *Philosophy in the Flesh: The Embodied Mind and its Challenge to Western Thought*, 13.

2. Ibid., p. 45.

3. de Bono, *I Am Right, You Are Wrong: From Rock Logic to Water Logic*, 103.

4. Merriam-Webster's Collegiate Dictionary, 10th ed. (Springfield, MA: Merriam-Webster, Inc., 1999), 233.

5. Lakoff and Johnson, *Philosophy in the Flesh: The Embodied Mind and its Challenge to Western Thought*, 47.

6. S.R. Axley, "Managerial and Organizational Communication in Terms of the Conduit Metaphor," *The Academy of Management Review* 9, no. 3 (1984): 428-437.

7. G. Lakoff, *Moral Politics: How Liberals and Conservatives Think* (Chicago: University of Chicago Press, 2002), 65-140.

8. S. McCorkle and J. Mills, "Rowboat in a Hurricane: Metaphors of Interpersonal Conflict Management," *Communication Reports* 5, no. 2 (1992): 57-66, cited in W. Wilmot and J. Hocker, *Interpersonal Conflict*, 7th ed., (Boston: McGraw-Hill, 2001), 17.

9. Ibid., 57-66.

10. T. A. Sowell, *A Conflict of Visions: Ideological Origins of Political*

Struggles (New York: William Morrow, 1987), quoted in M.D. Lang and A. Taylor, *The Making of a Mediator: Developing Artistry In Practice* (San Francisco: Jossey-Bass, 2000), 103-104.

11. Lakoff, *Moral Politics: How Liberals and Conservatives Think*, 65-140.
12. Sowell, *A Conflict of Visions: Ideological Origins of Political Struggles*, 103-104.
13. Lang and Taylor, *The Making of a Mediator: Developing Artistry in Practice*, 103-104.
14. C. Barks, *The Essential Rumi* (London: Penguin Books, 1995).
15. Mayer, *Beyond Neutrality: Confronting the Crisis in Conflict Resolution*, 129.
16. Ibid., 139-140.
17. Ibid., 289-291.
18. U. S. Army, *Living the Army Values* (GoArmy.com) http://www.goarmy.com/soldier-life/being-a-soldier/living-the-army-values.html
19. P. Loloi, *Hafiz, Master of Persian Poetry: A Critical Bibliography* (London: I.B. Tauris & Co, Ltd., 2004).

CHAPTER EIGHT – PICASSO MEETS THE RED QUEEN

1. L. Carroll, *Alice's Adventures in Wonderland* and *Through the Looking-Glass* (New York: Heritage Reprints, 1941), 115.
2. Lang and Taylor, *The Making of a Mediator: Developing Artistry in Practice*, 194.
3. American Psychiatric Association, *Diagnostic and Statistical Manual of Mental Disorders* (DSM-III-R) (Arlington, VA: American Psychiatric Publishing, Inc., 1987), 351.
4. S. Vaknin, *Malignant Self Love: Narcissism Revisited* (Skopje: Narcissus Publications & Lidija Rangelovska, 1999), 4. Author's website: http://samvak.tripod.com/
5. M. S. Peck, *People of the Lie: The Hope for Healing Human Evil* (New York: Simon & Schuster, 1983), 123.
6. A.T. Beck and A. Freedman *Cognitive Therapy of Personality Disorders* (New York: Guilford Press, 1990).

7. Vaknin, *Malignant Self Love: Narcissism Revisited*, 10.
8. Peck, *People of the Lie: The Hope for Healing Human Evil*, 42-43.
9. Ibid., 119.
10. Ibid., 121.
11. R. Fisher and S. Brown, *Getting Together: Building Relationships as We Negotiate* (New York: Penguin Books, 1988), 207-208.
12. W.A. Eddy, *High Conflict People in Legal Disputes* (San Diego, CA: HCI Press, 2006).
13. Lang and Taylor, *The Making of a Mediator: Developing Artistry in Practice*, 206.
14. Peck, *People of the Lie: The Hope for Healing Human Evil*, 123.

CHAPTER NINE – MEDIATION AS IMPROVISATION

1. Benjamin, "Managing the Natural Energy of Conflict: Mediators, Tricksters, and the Constructive Use of Deception," 79-134.
2. S. Colbert, *Knox College Commencement Address*, Knox College, Galesburg, IL, June 3, 2006. http://www.youtube.com/watch?v=lfWccASi6PM
3. K. Blanchard, P. Zigarmi, and D. Zigarmi, *Leadership and the One Minute Manager* (New York: William Morrow and Company, 1985), 1-2.
4. J.C. Peterson, *Why Don't We Listen Better? Communicating and Connecting in Relationships* (Portland, OR: Peterson Press, 2007), 10-17.
5. G. Lockwood, *Attention Please: May I Have Your Attention?* (BizSuccess.com, 2005). http://www.bizsuccess.com/articles/attention.htm
6. Fredrickson, *Positivity*, 69.
7. R.B. Maddux and B. Wingfield, *Team Building: An Exercise in Leadership*, 4th ed. (Menlo Park, CA: Crisp Learning, 2003).

CHAPTER TEN – IN DEFENSE OF CREATIVE PROBLEM SOLVING

1. S. Imperati, with D. Brownmiller and D. Marshall, "If Freud, Jung, Rogers, and Beck Were Mediators, Who Would the

Parties Pick and What are the Mediator's Obligations?" *Idaho Law Review* 43 (Spring, 2007): 1.

2. R.A.B Bush and J.P. Folger, *The Promise of Mediation: Responding to Conflict through Empowerment and Recognition* (San Francisco: Jossey-Bass, 1994).
3. Ibid., 12.
4. G. Puccio, M. Murdock, and M. Mance, *Creative Leadership: Skills That Drive Change* (Thousand Oaks, CA: Sage Publications, 2007), 37.
5. Ibid., 35.
6. G.A. Davis, *Creativity is Forever* (Dubuque, IA: Kendall/Hunt Publishing, 1986), 60.
7. C.H. Kepner and B.B. Tregoe, *The New Rational Manager* (Princeton, NJ: Princeton Research Press, 1981), 32.
8. W.J.J. Gordon, *Synectics: The Development of Creative Capacity* (New York: Harper & Row, 1961).
9. Ibid., 6-7.
10. Puccio, Murdock, and Mance, *Creative Leadership: Skills That Drive Change*, 25.
11. S.G. Isaksen, K.B. Dorval, and D.J. Treffinger, *Creative Approaches to Problem Solving* (Dubuque, IA: Kendall/Hunt Publishing, 1994), 44-47.
12. D.M. Kolb and J. Williams, *Everyday Negotiation: Navigating the Hidden Agendas in Bargaining* (San Francisco: Jossey-Bass, 2003), 288.
13. Isaksen, Dorval, and Treffinger, *Creative Approaches to Problem Solving*, 48-50.
14. Imperati, with Brownmiller and Marshall, "If Freud, Jung, Rogers, and Beck Were Mediators, Who Would the Parties Pick and What are the Mediator's Obligations?" 3.
15. Mayer, *Beyond Neutrality: Confronting the Crisis in Conflict Resolution*, 118.
16. L.J. Frech and L. Neilson, *Mediation Report: Rock Creek/Urban Growth Boundary Review* (Portland, OR, 2006).
17. B. Eberle, *SCAMPER: Creative Games and Activities for Imagination Development* (Waco, TX: Prufrock Press, 2008).

CHAPTER ELEVEN – THE AUTHOR'S DIALOGUE CREATIVELY CONTINUES

1. Mayer, *Beyond Neutrality: Confronting the Crisis in Conflict Resolution*, 213.
2. Lederach, *The Moral Imagination: The Art and Soul of Building Peace*, 174-175.
3. Lang and Taylor, *The Making of a Mediator: Developing Artistry in Practice*, 240-241.
4. Ibid., 83-84.
5. Mayer, *Beyond Neutrality: Confronting the Crisis in Conflict Resolution*, 217.
6. Csikszentmihalyi, *Creativity: Flow and the Psychology of Discovery and Invention*, 9.
7. G.E. Reed, *Needs: The Journey of How Interpersonal Conflict Produced Chances for Better Choices* (Portland, OR: Negotiating Shadows Publishing, 2010).
8. Ibid., i.
9. Ibid., 3.
10. J. Brooks, *The Changing Future of Mediation*, Presentation at the 20th anniversary celebration of the City of Beaverton Neighborhood Mediation Center, Beaverton, OR, September, 2008.
11. Ibid.
12. J. Mowry, *Restorative Justice: Repairing Harm to Create Common Ground*, Presentation at the Oregon Mediation Association Annual Conference, Oregon Convention Center, Portland, OR, November 7-8, 2008.

CHAPTER TWELVE – CONCLUSION

1. Mayer, *Beyond Neutrality: Confronting the Crisis in Conflict Resolution*, 295.
2. M. Williamson, *A Return to Love: Reflections on the Principles of a Course in Miracles* (New York: Harper Collins, 1992).
3. Mayer, *Beyond Neutrality: Confronting the Crisis in Conflict Resolution*, 295.

Bibliography

Ackerman, D. *The Alchemy of the Brain: The Marvel and Mystery of the Brain.* New York: Scribner, 2004.

Adams, J.L. *Conceptual Blockbusting: A Guide to Better Ideas.* 3rd ed. Reading, MA: Addison-Wesley Publishing Co., 1986.

Adler, P. "Unintentional Excellence: An Exploration of Mastery and Incompetence." In *Bringing Peace into the Room*, edited by D. Bowling and D. Hoffman, 57-75. San Francisco: Jossey-Bass, 2003.

American Psychiatric Association. *Diagnostic and Statistical Manual of Mental Disorders* (DSM-III-R). Arlington, VA: American Psychiatric Publishing, Inc., 1987.

Andreasen, N.C. *The Creating Brain: The Neuroscience of Genius.* New York: DanaPress, 2005.

Axley, S.R. "Managerial and Organizational Communication in Terms of the Conduit Metaphor." *The Academy of Management Review* 9, no. 3 (1984): 428-437.

Barks, C. *The Essential Rumi.* London: Penguin Books, 1995.

Beck, A.T., and Freedman, A. *Cognitive Therapy of Personality Disorders.* New York: Guilford Press, 1990.

Benjamin, R.D. "Managing the Natural Energy of Conflict: Mediators, Tricksters, and the Constructive Use of Deception." In *Bringing Peace into the Room*, edited by D. Bowling and D. Hoffman, 79-134. San Francisco: Jossey-Bass, 2003.

Blanchard, K., Zigarmi, P., and Zigarmi, D. *Leadership and the One Minute Manager.* New York: William Morrow and Company, 1985.

Blanchard, K., Carlos, J.P., and Randolph, A. *The Three Keys to Empowerment: Release the Power within People for Astonishing*

Results. San Francisco: Berrett-Koehler Publishers, 1999.

Block, J., and Kremen, A.M. "IQ and Ego-Resiliency: Conceptual and Empirical Connections and Separateness." *Journal of Personality and Social Psychology* 70, no. 2 (1996): 349-361.

Bowling, D., and Hoffman, D., eds. *Bringing Peace into the Room*. San Francisco: Jossey-Bass, 2003.

Brooks, J. *The Changing Future of Mediation*. Presentation at the 20th anniversary celebration of the City of Beaverton Neighborhood Mediation Center. Beaverton, OR, September, 2008.

Bush, R.A.B. and Folger, J.P. *The Promise of Mediation: Responding to Conflict through Empowerment and Recognition*. San Francisco: Jossey-Bass, 1994.

Cameron, J. *The Artist's Way: A Spiritual Path to Higher Creativity*. New York: Tarcher/Putnam, 1992.

Carne, G.C., and Kirton, M.J. "Styles of Creativity: Test-Score Correlations between the Kirton Adaption-Innovation Inventory and the Myers-Briggs Type Indicator." *Psychological Reports* 50 (1982): 31-36.

Carroll, L. *Alice's Adventures in Wonderland* and *Through the Looking-Glass*. New York: Heritage Reprints, 1941.

Cloke, K. *Mediating Dangerously: The Frontiers of Conflict Resolution*. San Francisco: Jossey-Bass, 2001.

Colbert, S. *Knox College Commencement Address*. Knox College, Galesburg, IL, June 3, 2006. http://www.youtube.com/watch?v=lfWccASi6PM

Csikszentmihalyi, M. *Creativity: Flow and the Psychology of Discovery and Invention*. New York: HarperCollins, 1996.

———. *Finding Flow: The Psychology of Engagement in Everyday Life*. New York: HarperCollins, 1997.

Davis, G.A. *Creativity is Forever*. Dubuque, IA: Kendall/Hunt, 1986.

de Bono, E. *I Am Right, You Are Wrong: From Rock Logic to Water Logic*. New York: Viking Penguin, 1991.

———. *de Bono's Thinking Course* (revised). New York: Facts on File, Inc., 1994.

Driscoll, J. "Defense Workers Shift Gears: Confronting Ethical Dilemmas in the Workplace." *Plowshares Press*, Autumn, 1988. Quoted in Louise Neilson, *Impact of Creative Problem Solving Training: An In Depth Evaluation of a Six Day Course in Creative Problem Solving* (Unpublished master's project. SUNY College of Buffalo, Buffalo, NY, 1990), 3.

Dryden, G., and Vos, J. *The Learning Revolution: A Lifelong Learning Programme for the World's Finest Computer: Your Amazing Brain!* Torrance, CA: Jalmar Press, 1994.

Eberle, B. *SCAMPER: Creative Games and Activities for Imagination Development*. Waco, TX: Prufrock Press, 2008.

Eddy, W.A. *High Conflict People in Legal Disputes*. San Diego, CA: HCI Press, 2006.

Eliot, T.S. "Little Gidding V." (1942). In *Collected Poems 1909-1962*. New York: Harcourt Brace, 1963.

Firestien, R.L. *Leading on the Creative Edge: Gaining Competitive Advantage Through the Power of Creative Problem Solving*. Colorado Springs, CO: Pinon Press, 1996.

Fisher, R., and Brown, S. *Getting Together: Building Relationships as We Negotiate*. New York: Penguin Books, 1988.

Frech, L.J., and Neilson, L. *Mediation Report: Rock Creek/Urban Growth Boundary Review*. Portland, OR, 2006.

Fredrickson, B.L. *Positivity*. New York: Crown Publishers, 2009.

Galton, F. "Hereditary Genius: An Inquiry into Its Laws and Consequences" (1869). In *The Creativity Question*, edited by A. Rothenberg and C.R. Hausman, 42-48. Durham, NC: Duke University Press, 1976.

Gardner, H. *Creating Minds: An Anatomy of Creativity as Seen through the Lives of Freud, Einstein, Picasso, Stravinsky, Eliot, Graham, and Gandhi*. New York: BasicBooks, 1993.

Gordon, W.J.J. *Synectics: The Development of Creative Capacity*. New York: Harper & Row, 1961.

Gottman, J.M. *What Predicts Divorce? The Relationship between Marital Processes and Marital Outcomes*. Hillsdale, NJ: Lawrence Erlbaum Associates, 1994.

Guilford, J.P. *Way Beyond the IQ: Guide to Improving Intelligence and Creativity.* Buffalo, NY: Creative Education Foundation, 1977.

———. "Creativity Research: Past, Present, Future." In *Frontiers of Creativity Research: Beyond the Basics,* edited by S.G. Isaksen, 33-65. Buffalo, NY: Bearly Limited, 1987.

Hafiz. *Hafiz, Master of Persian Poetry: A Critical Bibliography.* Translated by P. Loloi. London: I.B. Tauris & Co, Ltd., 2004. (Original work published circa 1350.)

Herrmann, N. *The Creative Brain.* Lake Lure, NC: Brain Books, 1989.

Hirsh, S.K., and Kummerow, J.M. *Introduction to Type in Organizations.* 3rd ed. Palo Alto, CA: Consulting Psychologists Press, 1998.

Imperati, S., with Brownmiller, D. and Marshall, D. "If Freud, Jung, Rogers, and Beck Were Mediators, Who Would the Parties Pick and What are the Mediator's Obligations?" *Idaho Law Review* 43 (Spring, 2007): 643-708.

Isaksen, S.G., ed. *Frontiers of Creativity Research: Beyond the Basics.* Buffalo, NY: Bearly Limited, 1987.

Isaksen, S.G., Dorval, K.B., and Treffinger, D.J. *Creative Approaches to Problem Solving.* Dubuque, IA: Kendall/Hunt Publishing, 1994.

Isaksen, S.G., and Treffinger, D.J. *Creative Problem Solving: The Basic Course.* Buffalo, NY: Bearly Limited, 1985.

Jaynes, J. *The Origins of Consciousness in the Breakdown of the Bicameral Mind.* Boston: Houghton Mifflin, 1976.

Johnston, C.M. *The Creative Imperative: Human Growth and Planetary Evolution.* Berkeley, CA: Celestial Arts, 1986.

Kelly, A.E., and McKillop, K.J. "Consequences of Revealing Personal Secrets." *Psychological Bulletin* 120, no. 3 (1996): 450.

Kepner, C.H., and Tregoe, B.B. *The New Rational Manager.* Princeton, NJ: Princeton Research Press, 1981.

Kirton, M.J. "Adaptors and Innovators: A Description and Measure." *Journal of Applied Psychology* 61, no. 5 (1976): 622-629.

———, ed. *Adaptors and Innovators: Styles of Creativity and Problem*

Solving. London: Routledge, 1994.

———— *Adaption-Innovation: In the Context of Diversity and Change*. London: Routledge, 2003.

Koestler, A. *Insight and Outlook: An Inquiry into Common Foundations of Science, Art and Social Ethics*. Lincoln, NB: University of Nebraska Press, 1949.

———— *The Act of Creation*. New York: Dell Publishing Company, 1964.

Kolb, D.M., and Williams, J. *Everyday Negotiation: Navigating the Hidden Agendas in Bargaining*. San Francisco: Jossey-Bass, 2003.

Kris, E. "On Preconscious Mental Processes" (1952). In *The Creativity Question*, edited by A. Rothenberg and C.R. Hausman, 135-143. Durham, NC: Duke University Press, 1976.

Kroeger, O., and Thuesen, J.M. *Type Talk*. New York: Delacorte Press, 1988.

Kubie, L.S. "Creation and Neurosis" (1958). In *The Creativity Question*, edited by A. Rothenberg and C.R. Hausman, 143-148. Durham, NC: Duke University Press, 1976.

Lakoff, G., and Johnson, M. *Metaphors We Live By*. Chicago: University of Chicago Press, 1980.

———— *Philosophy in the Flesh: The Embodied Mind and Its Challenge to Western Thought*. New York: Basic Books, 1999.

Lakoff, G. *Moral Politics: How Liberals and Conservatives Think*. Chicago: University of Chicago Press, 2002.

Lang, M.D., and Taylor, A. *The Making of a Mediator: Developing Artistry in Practice*. San Francisco: Jossey-Bass, 2000.

LeBaron, M. *Bridging Troubled Waters: Conflict Resolution from the Heart*. San Francisco: Jossey-Bass, 2002.

———— "Trickster, Mediator's Friend." In *Bringing Peace into the Room*, edited by D. Bowling and D. Hoffman, 135-150. San Francisco: Jossey-Bass, 2003.

Lederach, J.P. *The Moral Imagination: The Art and Soul of Building Peace*. New York: Oxford University Press, 2005.

Lockwood, G. *Attention Please: May I Have Your Attention?* BizSuccess.com, 2005. http://www.bizsuccess.com/articles/attention.htm

Loloi, P. *Hafiz, Master of Persian Poetry: A Critical Bibliography*. London: I.B. Tauris & Co, Ltd, 2004.

Lombroso, C. "Genius and Insanity" (1895). In *The Creativity Question*, edited by A. Rothenberg and C.R. Hausman, 79-86. Durham, NC: Duke University Press, 1976.

Loomis, M.E. *Dancing the Wheel of Psychological Types*. Wilmette, IL: Chiron, 1991.

Luft, J. *Of Human Interaction*. Palo Alto, CA: National Press, 1969.

––––––– *Group Processes: An Introduction to Group Dynamics*. 5th ed. Palo Alto, CA: National Press Books, 1970.

MacKinnon, D.W. "Architects, Personality Types, and Creativity" (1965). In *The Creativity Question*, edited by A. Rothenberg and C.R. Hausman, 175-189. Durham, NC: Duke University Press, 1976.

McBroom, A., and Goldman, C. "The Sticky Middle Part: Between the Opening Statement and Agreements." Bellevue, Washington Neighborhood Mediation Program *Update*, January, 2000.

McCorkle, S., and Mills, J. "Rowboat in a Hurricane: Metaphors of Interpersonal Conflict Management." *Communication Reports* 5, no. 2 (1992): 57-66.

Maddux, R.B., and Wingfield, B. *Team Building: An Exercise in Leadership*. 4th ed. Menlo Park, CA: Crisp Learning, 2003.

Maslow, A.H. *Toward a Psychology of Being*. 2nd ed. Princeton, NJ: VanNostrand, 1968.

––––––– *The Farther Reaches of Human Nature*. New York: Viking Press, 1971.

Mayer, B.S. *Beyond Neutrality: Confronting the Crisis in Conflict Resolution*. San Francisco: Jossey-Bass, 2004.

Mowry, J. *Restorative Justice: Repairing Harm to Create Common Ground*. Presentation at the Oregon Mediation Association Annual Conference, Oregon Convention Center, Portland, OR, November 7-8, 2008.

Murray, W.H. *The Scottish Himalayan Expedition*. London: Dent, 1951.

Myers, I.B. *Gifts Differing*. Palo Alto, CA: Consulting Psychologists Press, 1986.

Myers, I.B., McCaulley, M.H., Quenk, N.L., and Hammer, A.L. *Manual: A Guide to the Development and Use of the Myers-Briggs Type Indicator*. 3rd ed. Palo Alto, CA: Consulting Psychologists Press, 1998.

Nachmanovitch, S. *Free Play: The Power of Improvisation in Life and the Arts*. New York: Putnam & Sons, 1990.

Neilson, L. *Impact of Creative Problem Solving Training: An In Depth Evaluation of a Six Day Course in Creative Problem Solving*. Unpublished master's project. SUNY College of Buffalo, Buffalo, NY, 1990.

Novello, D. "The Five Minute University" (1979). On *Gilda, Live!* Warner Bros., 2009. http://www.youtube.com/watch?v=kO8x8eoU3L4

Organisation for Economic Co-operation and Development. *Understanding the Brain: The Birth of a Learning Science*. Paris, France: Centre for Educational Research and Innovation, 2007.

Parnes, S. "The Creative Studies Project" (1973). In *Frontiers of Creativity Research: Beyond the Basics*, edited by S.G. Isaksen, 156-188. Buffalo, NY: Bearly Limited, 1987.

Pearman, R.R., and Albritton, S.C. *I'm Not Crazy, I'm Just Not You: The Real Meaning of the Sixteen Personality Types*. Palo Alto, CA: Davis-Black, 1997.

Peck, M.S. *People of the Lie: The Hope for Healing Human Evil*. New York: Simon & Schuster, 1983.

Peterson, J.C. *Why Don't We Listen Better? Communicating and Connecting in Relationships*. Portland, OR: Peterson Press, 2007.

Pitts, L. "Ignore the Facts, If Your Mind Is Made Up." *The Miami Herald*, April 16, 2007.

Puccio, G.J., Murdock, M.C., and Mance, M. *Creative Leadership: Skills That Drive Change*. Thousand Oaks, CA: Sage Publications, 2007.

Rank, O. "Life and Creation" (1932). In *The Creativity Question*, edited by A. Rothenberg and C.R. Hausman, 114-120. Durham, NC: Duke University Press, 1976.

Ratey, J.J. *A User's Guide to The Brain: Perception, Attention, and the Four Theaters of the Brain.* New York: Vintage Books, 2002.

Reed, G.E. *Needs: The Journey of How Interpersonal Conflict Produced Chances for Better Choices.* Portland, OR: Negotiating Shadows Publishing, 2010.

Reitman, J.W. "The Personal Qualities of the Mediator: Taking Time for Reflection and Renewal." In *Bringing Peace into the Room,* edited by D. Bowling and D. Hoffman, 235-244. San Francisco: Jossey-Bass, 2003.

Rogers, E. *Diffusion of Innovations.* 4th ed. New York: Simon and Schuster, 1995.

Rothenberg, A., and Hausman, C.R., eds. *The Creativity Question.* Durham, NC: Duke University Press, 1976.

Rowe, J. "In Review: From Raising Hell to Raising Barns." *Yes!* 46 (Summer, 2008). http://www.yesmagazine.org/issues/a-just-foreign-policy/in-review-from-raising-hell-to-raising-barns

Rudkin, D., Allan, D., Murrin, K., and Kingdon, M. (?What If!) *Sticky Wisdom: How to Start a Creative Revolution at Work.* Oxford, UK: Capstone Publishing Limited, 2002.

Saposnek, D. "Style and the Family Mediator." In *Bringing Peace into the Room,* edited by D. Bowling and D. Hoffman, 245-256. San Francisco: Jossey-Bass, 2003.

Schell, J. "The Fate of the Earth" New York: Alfred A. Knopf, 1982, 188. Quoted in Louise Neilson, *Impact of Creative Problem Solving Training: An In Depth Evaluation of a Six Day Course in Creative Problem Solving* (Unpublished master's project. SUNY College of Buffalo, Buffalo, NY, 1990), 2.

Seligman, M.E.P. and Csikszentmihalyi, M. "Positive Psychology: An Introduction." *American Psychologist* 55, no. 1 (2000): 5-14. Cited in B.L. Fredrickson, *Positivity* (New York: Crown Publishers, 2009), 181.

Senge, P., Scharmer, C.O., Jaworski, J., and Flowers, B.S. *Presence: An Exploration of Profound Change in People, Organizations, and Society.* New York: Doubleday, 2005.

Shirky, C. *Cognitive Surplus: Creativity and Generosity in a Connected*

Age. New York: Penguin Group, 2010.

Sowell, T. A. *A Conflict of Visions: Ideological Origins of Political Struggles.* New York: William Morrow, 1987. Quoted in M.D. Lang and A. Taylor, *The Making of a Mediator: Developing Artistry in Practice* (San Francisco: Jossey-Bass Publishers, 2000), 103-104.

Torrance, E.P. "Scientific Views of Creativity and Factors Affecting Its Growth" (1965). In *The Creativity Question,* edited by A. Rothenberg and C.R. Hausman, 217-227. Durham, NC: Duke University Press, 1976.

———. *The Search for Satori and Creativity.* Buffalo, NY: Creative Education Foundation, 1979.

Treffinger, D.J., Isaksen, S.G., and Dorval, K.B. *Creative Problem Solving: An Introduction.* 3rd ed. Waco, TX: Prufrock Press, 2000.

Ulrich, D. *The Widening Stream: The Seven Stages of Creativity.* Hillsboro, OR: Beyond Words Publishing, 2002.

Ury, W., and Fisher, R. *Getting Past No: Negotiating with Difficult People.* New York: Bantam Books, 1999.

U.S. Army. *Living the Army Values.* GoArmy.com. http://www.goarmy.com/soldier-life/being-a-soldier/living-the-army-values.html

Vaknin, S. *Malignant Self Love: Narcissism Revisited.* Skopje: Narcissus Publications & Lidija Rangelovska, 1999. Author's website: http://samvak.tripod.com/

Wade, L. "Mediation and Personality Type." *Mediation Monthly* (August 1996): 4-5.

Weisbord, M.R. *Discovering Common Ground.* San Francisco: Berrett-Koehler, 1992.

Wheatley, M.J. *Turning to One Another: Simple Conversations to Restore Hope to the Future.* San Francisco: Berrett-Koehler, 2002.

Williamson, M. *A Return to Love: Reflections on the Principles of a Course in Miracles.* New York: Harper Collins, 1992.

Index

Page references in italics indicate illustrations, graphics, excerpts on even-numbered (left-hand) pages.

Adaption-Innovation: In the Context of Diversity and Change (Kirton), *104, 106*
Adaptive creative style (KAI), 99, 101, 103, *106*, 127
adaptive type (Rank), 91
affirmative judgment, *216*
"aha" moments, 25, 27, 71, 79
Alice (in Wonderland), *162*, 163, *166*, 170, 172, 176
Alice's Adventures in Wonderland (Carroll), *176*
Allan, Dave, *94*
Allen, Woody, 87
alpha brain waves, 47, 57
Alternative Dispute Resolution department (Better Business Bureau), 71, 149, 183
ambiguity, 21, 47, 107
androgyny, psychological, 53
architects, 31, 33, 35, 43
"Architects, Personality Types, and Creativity" (MacKinnon), *30*
Aristotle, 89, 99
Army Values, 153, *154*, 155
The Artist's Way: A Spiritual Path to Higher Creativity (Cameron), 164
artist type (Rank), 91

attributes of creative people
   integrated yet opposing, 47–55
   most characteristic, *30*
   self-actualized assessment, *34*
   skill, motivation, ability as, *44*
attributes (four) of creativity, 45
attributes of mediators, 21, 33, *118, 196*. See also mediators.
attributes of mental health, *92*, 93
Axley, Stephen R., *138*

barriers to creative thinking
   childhood experiences, 61
   mental blind spots (scotomas), 63, 65, 67
   negativity, 59, 61, 67, 69
Beaverton, Oregon, Dispute Resolution Center, 231, 233, 235
belief systems, 27, 61, 81, *84*, 149
Benjamin, Robert D., *196*
beta brain waves, 47, 57
Better Business Bureau, Alternative Dispute Resolution department, 71, 149, 183
Beyond Neutrality: Confronting the Crisis in Conflict Resolution (Mayer), 11, *20*, 21, *150, 152, 212, 218, 226, 232*

bisociative thinking, 21, 47
Blanchard, Kenneth H., 187, *188*, 189, *190*, *192*
Blind Area, 75–81
Blinding Flash of the Obvious (BFO), 31, 33, 79, 123, 205, 223, 237
blocks. *See also* mental blocks.
   cultural, 73, 76
   emotional, 75
   family-of-origin, 83
   perceptual, 74, 75
   personal, *82*
boundaries, 49, *180*
Bowling, Daniel, *56*, *58*, *108*, *178*, *180*
brain information processing, *14*, 25, 41, 87
Bridging Troubled Waters (LeBaron), 72
Bringing Peace into the Room (Bowling & Hoffman), *56*, *58*, *108*, *178*, *180*
Brooks, Jim, 233, 235
Brown, Scott, *168*, *174*
Buff State College (Buffalo, New York), 95
Bush, R.A.B., 201

Cameron, Julia, *164*
Carlos, John P., *190*, *192*
Carroll, Lewis, 159, *162*, 163, *166*, 170, *172*, 176
catchment words, 137, 139, 199
Chances for Choices Project, 229, 231
"The Children of the Other Shoe," 231
Clarification stage of CPS Thinking Skills model, *202*, 203
coaching leadership, 191
Coach persona, 191, 193
Cognitive Surplus: Creativity and Generosity in a Connected Age (Shirky), *228*
Colbert, Stephen, 179, 181

competency in mediation, 19, 21
conduit metaphor, 139, *142*, 143
conflict, 11, *114*, 163, 197
conflict resolution, 13, 15, 21, *212*
conflict specialists, 223, 231, *232*, 235
connectivity, 67
"Consequences of Revealing Personal Secrets (Kelly & McKillop)", 70
convergent thinking, 45, 207, 211, 213, 215
coping mechanisms, 161
coping skills, 109
Corcoran, Kevin, 153, 155
courage and creativity, 94
Coyote, 21, 179
CPS. *See* Creative Problem Solving (CPS).
crazymakers (Cameron), 164
"Creation and Neurosis" (Kubie), 92
Creative Approaches to Problem Solving (Isaksen, Dorval & Treffinger), *216*
Creative Assessment Summary, 17
The Creative Brain (Herrmann), 14, 91
Creative Imperative: Human Growth and Planetary Evolution (Johnston), *182*
Creative Leadership: Skills That Drive Change (Puccio, Murdock & Mance), *116*, *200*, *202*, *208*
creative "press" (or environment), 43, 45
Creative Problem Solving (CPS)
   course work about, 13, 59, 95
   divergent thinking and, 207, 209
   ground rules, 209, 211
   mediation and, 199, 205, *206*, 207, 223
   and mediation hybrid, 215,

217, 219
original model of, 203
stages of, 202, 203, 208
Creative Problem Solving: An Introduction (Treffinger, Isaksen & Dorval), 88
Creative Problem Solving: The Basic Course (Isaksen & Treffinger), 210, 214
Creative Problem Solving: The Thinking Skills Model, 201, 202, 203
Creative Problem Solving Institute, Chicago, 79
Creative Problem Solving Workshop format, 217
creative products, 43, 45
Creative Styles Workshops, 109
creativity
    approaches to, 46
    in architects, 31, 33, 35, 43
    basic concepts of, 43
    conflict situations and, 11, 15, 21, 212
    confusion and, 240
    convergent decision making aspect of, 211
    courage and, 94
    four attributes of, 45, 207, 209
    historical attitudes toward, 87–97
    inherent individual, 9, 11, 43
    kinds of, 32
    level of, 98
    mental illness and, 89–93
    metaphors and, 141, 149
    misconceptions of, 88
    origins of, 87, 89
    problem solving and, 199
    processes of, 45, 87, 89, 93, 201
    products of, 43, 45, 89
    social conditions and, 224, 225
    styles of, 98, 99–109, 197
    as teachable, 95
    theories and perspectives, 43, 45
Creativity: Flow and the Psychology of Discovery and Invention (Csikszentmihalyi), 50, 184, 224
Creativity and Innovation Management Conference, 81
Creativity is Forever (Davis), 74, 76, 82
Csikszentmihalyi, Mihaly, 47, 49, 50, 55, 184, 224
cultural boundaries, 73
cultural conflicts, 11

Damon, Jamie, 83
Darwin, Charles, 89
Davis, Gary, 74, 76, 82
de Bono, Edward, 21
decision making guidelines, 214
"Defense Workers Shift Gears" (Driscoll), 10
delegating leadership, 195, 197
"determined" aspect of creativity, 89, 99
Diagnostic and Statistical Manual of Mental Disorders, 160, 161
directing leadership, 189
directive problem solving, 201
directive Settlement Conference model, 189
DiscoverYourPersonality.com, 113
divergent thinking, 45, 207, 209, 211
diversity, psychological, 116
diversity of problems, 104
Dorval, K. Brian, 88, 216
Driscoll, J., 10
Dryden, Gordon, 14, 40

Eddy, W.A. "Bill," 173
Educators for Social Responsibility,

13
Ego-Resiliency Scale, 125
Einstein, Albert, 11, 237
elaboration attribute, 45, 209
Eliot, T.S., 236
empowerment, 187, 189, 190
English language and metaphors, 135
extraversion, 51
Extraversion/Introversion Scale, 113
Extraverts (E), 113, 115

The Farther Reaches of Human Nature (Maslow), 34, 48
Father Guido Sarducci (Saturday Night Live), 43
Feeling (F), 119, 121
Firestien, Roger, 6
Fisher, Roger, 168, 174
Five Minute University, 43
flat brains, 191, 193, 194
flexibility attribute, 45, 209
"flow" (optimal experience), 21, 55, 57
fluency attribute, 45, 207, 209
Folger, J.P., 201
Fredrickson, Barbara L., 36, 38, 41, 66, 68, 125, 238
Free Play: The Power of Improvisation in Life and the Arts (Nachmanovitch), 18, 198
Freud, Sigmund, 91
"From Raising Hell to Raising Barns" (Rowe), 78

Galton, Francis, 89, 91
gender
    differences between Thinkers/Feelers, 119, 121
    metaphors and, 147
    role stereotyping, 53
"Genius and Insanity" (Lombroso), 90
Getting Together: Building Relationships as We Negotiate (Fisher & Brown), 168, 174
Gandhi, 47
Gifts Differing (Myers), 112
glossary of terms, 245–47
Gottman, John, 69
Guardians, 120
Guilford, J.P., 46

Hafiz, Sufi Master, 157
Hammer, Allen L., 110, 118, 120
Hannan, Karen, 183
hardwired metaphors, 135, 139, 147
hemispheres of brain, 14, 41, 43, 51
hereditary degeneration, signs of, 90, 91
Herrmann, Ned, 14, 89, 91
Hidden Area, 73, 75, 81, 141
hierarchy of needs (Maslow), 33
High Conflict People in Legal Disputes (Eddy), 173
Hirsh, Sandra K., 128
historical attitudes toward creativity, 87–97
Hoffman, David, 56, 58, 108, 178, 180
hybrid CPS/mediation approach, 215, 217, 219

idea generating guidelines, 209, 210, 211
Idealists, 118
imagination, 21, 228
I'm Not Crazy, I'm Just Not You (Pearman & Albritton), 122
impartiality, 133, 137, 149, 181
Imperati, Sam, 79
Implementation stage of CPS Thinking Skills model, 202, 203, 205
improvisation, 179, 181
Innovative creative style (KAI), 99, 101, 103, 105, 127

Introduction to Type in Organizations (Hirsh & Kummerow), 128
introversion, 51
Introverts (I), 113, 115
intuition, *86*, 171
Intuitives (N), 115, 117, 127
Inventory, Values, 133
IQ (intelligence quotient), 49
Isaksen, Scott G., 88, *210*, *214*, *216*

Jaynes, Julian, 87
Johari Window
    Blind Area, 75–81
    Hidden Area, 73, 75, 81, 141
    Open Area, 71, 73, 79, 81, 85
    Unknown Area, 71, 73, 141
Johnson, Mark, *132*, *136*
Judging (J), 121, 123, 127
Judgment/Perception Scale, 121, 127
juggling type theory, 129, *130*, 131
Jung, Carl, 111, 119

KAI. *See* Kirton Adaption-Innovation Inventory (KAI).
Kepner-Tregoe Model, 201
Kirton, Michael, 103, *104*, 106, 107
Kirton Adaption-Innovation Inventory (KAI), *98*, 99, 105, 107, 127
Koestler, Arthur, 47
Kris, Ernst, 93
Kroeger, Otto, *114*
Kubie, Lawrence, *92*, 93
Kummerow, Jean M., *128*

Lakoff, George, *132*, *136*, *142*, *143*, *144*, *148*
Lang, Michael D. & Alison Taylor
    awareness of underlying principles, on, *26*, *64*, *156*
    intuition as artistry, on, *86*
    mediation as a creative process, on, *146*
    metaphors and mediation, on, *147*, 149
    recommendations for changes, on, 23
    strategic thinking for mediators, on, 21
    transforming the field, on, 221, 223
lateral thinking, 21
leadership
    coaching, 191, 193
    delegating, 195
    directing, 189, 191
    situational, 187, *188*, 189
    supporting, 189, 193, 195
Leadership and the One Minute Manager (Blanchard, Zigarmi, Zigarmi), *188*
leadership styles, 189
Leading on the Creative Edge (Firestien), 6
learning, whole brain, 15
The Learning Revolution (Dryden & Vos), 14, 40
LeBaron, Michelle, 72
Lederach, John Paul, 8, 9, *52*, 54, 221, 223
level of creativity, *98*
Literalist persona, *183*, *185*
"Little Gidding" (Eliot), *236*
Little Sister persona, 181, *183*, *185*
Lombroso, Cesare, 89, *90*, 91
Longfellow, Henry Wadsworth, 99
Luigi chat, 43
Luigi's notes on creativity, *42*

MacKinnon, Donald, *30*, 31, *33*, 35
Making of a Mediator: Developing Artistry in Practice (Lang & Taylor), 23, *26*, *64*, *86*, *146*, *156*
Managerial and Organizational Communication in Terms of the Conduit Metaphor, *138*

Mance, Marie, 116, 200, 202, 208
Manual: A Guide to the Development and Use of the Myers-Briggs Type Indicator (Myers, McCaulley, Quenk & Hammer), 110, 118, 120. See also MBTI Manual.
Marylhurst University, 71
Maslow, Abraham
  creativity and mental illness, on, 93
  hierarchy of needs, on, 33
  kinds of creativity, on, 32
  self-actualization, on, 33, 34, 35, 37, 47, 48
  self-actualizing creativity, on, 32, 33, 35
  traits of creative people, on, 34, 49
Mayer, Bernard
  challenges to the field, on, 11, 239
  conflict and creative problem solving, on, 212
  creativity and mediators, on, 21
  effective marketing, on, 226
  effective problem solving activities, on, 218
  full utilization of mediation services, on, 223
  mediation norms, on, 150, 151, 153
  methods to assist in conflict resolution, on, 232
  questioning belief systems, on, 84
  transformation of mediation field, on, 221, 223
  understanding approach to conflict, on, 20
  values about conflict, on, 152
MBTI. See Myers Briggs Type Indicator.
MBTI applications to mediation, 124, 129, 131
MBTI for Mediators Workshops, 111, 117, 121, 123, 125
MBTI Manual, 111
McCaulley, Mary H., 110, 118, 120
McKillop, Kevin, 70
meat grinder metaphor, 63, 75, 77, 93, 139
Mediating Dangerously: The Frontiers of Conflict Resolution (Cloke), 12
MediatingwithPicasso.com, 227
Mediating with Picasso Workbook, 17, 19, 37, 65, 111, 133, 155, 225
mediation
  community, 11
  creative problem solving and, 205, 206, 207, 213
  flow experiences and, 57
  as a giant puzzle, 204
  idea generating guidelines and, 209–11
  impartiality and, 133, 149, 181
  as improvisation, 179
  MBTI applications to, 124, 129, 131
  metaphors and, 7, 9, 141, 143, 145
  models, 189
  positivity and, 39
  process, 15, 43, 45, 137, 146
  skills, 17, 19, 21
  style, 197
"Mediation and Personality Type" (Wade), 126
mediators
  attributes of, 21, 33, 118, 196
  competencies of, 19, 21
  creative, 7, 31, 35, 41, 51, 55
  knowledge of constellation of theories, 156
  new, 17, 19
  norms of, 150

"outside the box" strategies and, 29
as peacemakers, *180*
personality type and, 127, 129, 131
preference for type, 125
style and, *100*
as trickster, *180*
values and, 133, *150*, 155, 157
memories, 23, *24*, 25
mental blind spots. *See* scotomas.
mental blocks, 71–85. *See also* Johari Window.
mental frames (metaphors), 141, 143, 147, 155
mental illness and creativity, 89–93
mental snow globe, 22, 23
metaphorical imagination, *132*
metaphors
    acquisition of, 135, *136*
    catchment words as, 137, 139, 199
    conduit, 139, *142*, 143
    for convergent and divergent thinking, 207
    in English language, 135, 139
    hardwired, 135, 139, 147
    meat grinder, 63, 75, 77, 93, 139
    mediation and, 7, 9, 141, 143, 145
    on the mind, *134*
    morality and, 144, 145, 147
    primary. *See* primary metaphors
    usefulness of, 135
    values and, 133, 137
Metaphors We Live By (Lakoff & Johnson), *132*, *142*
Middle creative style (KAI), 107, 127
Minard, Julien, 55
misconceptions of creativity, *88*

The Moral Imagination (Lederach), 8, *52*, 54
morality and metaphor, 144, 145, 147
Moral Politics: How Liberals and Conservatives Think (Lakoff), *144*, 148
Mowry, Judith, 235
Murdock, Mary, *116*, *200*, *202*, *208*
Murray, W.H., 96
Murrin, Kris, 94
Muses, 87, 91
Myers, Isabel Briggs, *110*, *112*, *118*, *120*
Myers Briggs Type Indicator (MBTI), 111, 113, 119, *122*, 127

Nachmanovitch, Stephen, *18*, *198*
"Naked Truth about Problem Solving" workshop, 199, 201
narcissistic personality disorder, *160*, 161, 163, 165. *See also* Red Queens (RQs).
Needs: The Journey of How Interpersonal Conflict Produced Chances for Better Choices (Reed), 230
negativity, 67, 68, 69
neurotic type (Rank), 91
NF temperament: Idealist, *118*
nine dot puzzle, *28*, 29
norms, social, 73, *150*, 151
Nurturing Parent metaphor, 143, 147, 148, 149, 153

Open Area (Window), 71, 73, 79, 81, 85
optimal experience ("flow"), 21, 55, 57
Oregon Mediation Association, 199
originality attribute, 45, 209
"outside the box" thinking, 29

INDEX | 277

peacemaking, 11, 21, *180*, 239
Perman, Roger R., *122*
Peck, Morgan Scott, 165, 175
People of the Lie: The Hope for Healing Human Evil (Peck), 165
Perceiving (P), 121, 123, 127
personality disorders, 161
personality type instruments, 111
personality types (MBTI), 111–31
personas
    Coach, 191, 193
    Literalist, 183, 185
    Little Sister, 181, 183, 185
    Substitute Teacher, 181, 183, 187, 189
    trickster, 181
    Wall, 185, 187
Peterson, Jim, 191
Philosophy in the Flesh: The Embodied Mind and Its Challenge to Western Thought (Lakoff & Johnson), *136*
Picasso, Pablo, 7, 9, 49, 53, *186*
Picasso mind, 19
Plato, 87, 89, 91, 99
Portland, Oregon, Effective Engagement Solutions Program, 235
Portland Police Bureau, 227
Portland State University (PSU), 13, 95, 231
positive psychology, 37
positivity
    as contagious, 193
    creative mediators and, 41
    definition of, 39
    as essential to personal growth, 67
    opposing creative traits and, 47
    positive psychology and, 37
    as renewable, *238*
    resilent personalities and, 125
    words that reflect, *38*
Positivity (Fredrickson), *36*, *38*, 39, 66, 68, 125, *238*
positivity/negativity ratio, 67, 69
PositivityRatio.com, 69
preferences for type (Myers Briggs Type Indicator), *110*, 119, 121, *128*
press (or environment) of creativity, 43, 45
primary metaphors
    creativity and, 149
    impartiality and, 149
    scotomas, Unknown Area and, 141
    use of, *136*
    values and unconscious, 133, 135
    world view and, 143, 147
prince of paradox (wise fool), *182*
problem solving, 199. *See also* Creative Problem Solving (CPS).
products of creativity, 43, 45, 89
The Promise of Mediation, 199
psychological androgyny, 53
psychological diversity, 116
Puccio, Gerard, 116, 200, 202, 208

Quenk, Naomi L., *110*, *118*, *120*

radical creativity, 89, 107. *See also* "undetermined" aspect of creativity.
Randolph, Alan, *190*, *192*
Rank, Otto, 91, 93
Ratey, John J., *140*
RAS. *See* Reticular Activating System (RAS).
Red Queens (RQs)
    characteristics of, *160*, 163
    healthy narcissism vs., 175
    manipulation and exploitation by, 159

in mediation situations, 169
as narcissistic personalities, 161
personas and, 185
questions for potential responses by, *174*
strategies for confronting, *168*, 173
Reed, Grace E., 229, *230*, 231
Reticular Activating System (RAS)
CPS ground rules and, 209
functions and process of, 25, 63, 159, 171
metaphors and, 135
patterns and symbol recognition by, 63, 65
positivity and, 39
SCAMPER and, 217
scotomas (mental blocks) and, 85, 141
Synectics and, 203
reticular formation, 25
RQs. See Red Queens (RQs).
Rudkin, Daz, 94
Rumi, 151

Saposnek, Donald, *100*
SCAMPER, 217, 227
"Scientific Views of Creativity and Factors Affecting its Growth" (Torrance), *80*
scotomas (mental blind spots), 27, 29, 75, 141, 147, 149, 191. See also barriers to creative thinking; Reticular Activating System (RAS).
The Scottish Himalayan Expedition (Murray), 96
The Search for Satori and Creativity (Torrance), 44
self-actualization, 33, *34*, 35, 37, 47, *48*
self-actualizing creativity, *32*, 33, 35
self-assessment surveys, 17, 37
Seligman, Martin, 37
Senge, Peter, *222*
Sensing/Intuition Scale, 115, 127
Sensing (S) people, 115, 117, 127
Settlement Conference model, 189
settlement conferences, 201
Shirky, Clay, *228*
situational leadership, 187, *188*, 189, 197
SJ Temperament: Guardian, *120*
Snow Globe Theory, 23, 25
social conditions and creativity, *224*, 225
social norms, 73, *150*, 151
Sowell, Thomas A., 147
special talent creativeness, *32*, 33
Sticky Wisdom: How to Start a Creative Revolution at Work (Rudkin, Allan, Murrin & Kingdon), 94
Strict Father metaphor, 143, *144*, 145, 147, 149, 153, 189
"Style and the Family Mediator" (Saposnek), *100*
styles of creativity, 99–109, 125
style vs. level of creativity, 98
Substitute Teacher persona, 181, 183, 187, 189
supporting leadership, 189, 193, 195
Synectics model, 201, 203

Talented and Gifted (TAG) children, 13, 15
Taylor, Alison. See Lang, Michael D. & Alison Taylor.
Teufel, Judy, 225
Theory of Obnoxious People, 185
thinking. See also barriers to creative thinking.
lateral, 21

INDEX | 279

"outside the box," 29
whole brain, 21
Thinking (T), 119, 121
Thinking/Feeling Scale, 119
The Three Keys to Empowerment: Release the Power within People for Astonishing Results (Blanchard, Carlos & Randolph), *190, 192*
Through the Looking-Glass (Carroll), *159, 162, 163, 166, 170, 172*
Thuesen, Janet M., *114*
Torrance, E. Paul, 43, 44, 80
Toward a Psychology of Being (Maslow), 32
Townsend, Jon, 133, 173
traits. See attributes of creative people; attributes of mediators.
Transformation stage of CPS Thinking Skills model, 202, 203
Treffinger, Donald J., *88, 210, 214, 216*
trickster, 21, 179, 180, 181. See also Coyote.
Turning to One Another: Simple Conversations to Restore Hope to the Future (Wheatley), *240*
Type Talk (Kroeger & Thuesen), *114*
type theory, 122, 129

Ulrich, David, *220, 234*
"undetermined" aspect of creativity, 87, 89, 99
Unknown Area, 71, 73, 141
Urban Growth Boundary (UGB), Portland, Oregon, 215
User's Guide to the Brain: Perception, Attention, and the Four Theaters of the Brain (Ratey), *140*
values
about conflict, 152
Army, 153, 155
catchment metaphor and, 137
mediation literature and, 151, 153
mediators and, 133, 150, 155, 157
primary metaphors and, 143
Values Inventory, 133, 155
Vos, Jeannette, 14, 40

Wade, Lyn, *126*
Wall persona, 185, 187
Way Beyond the I.Q. (Guilford), *46*
Wheatley, Margaret J., *240*
Whitman, Walt, 99
whole brain learning, 15
whole brain thinking, 21, 239
The Widening Stream: The Seven Stages of Creativity (Ulrich), *220, 234*
Willamette University Law School Center for Dispute Resolution, 15
Workbook (Mediating with Picasso), 17, 19, 37, 65, 111, 133, 155, 225
world view, 143, 147
www.DiscoverYourPersonality.com, 113
www.MediatingwithPicasso.com, 227
www.PositivityRatio.com, 69

Yeung, Olivia, *204*

About the Author

Louise Neilson is the only mediator in the U.S. with a master's degree in Creativity and Innovation. Since 1990 she has taught creativity and conflict resolution courses at Marylhurst University. Concurrently, she has mediated over 1200 cases: complex workplace disputes for employee assistance programs, buyer/seller disputes while ADR Coordinator at the Better Business Bureau, neighborhood disputes for community programs, evictions and small claims cases for Multnomah County District Court, police/citizen cases for the City of Portland, and Equal Employment Opportunity Commission (EEOC) cases for the US Postal Service.

Louise was introduced to conflict resolution as a young adult; her husband was her boss while she supervised her mother-in-law. During her checkered past, Louise taught gifted inner city middle-schoolers, owned a specialty ceramic tile wholesale production company, taught resume-writing to out-placed factory workers, and organized dress-up nights and Ping-Pong tournaments at an annual residential art camp. Louise currently teaches, mediates, and doodles in the Portland, Oregon area.

Made in the USA
Monee, IL
16 November 2020